Alaska

& Yukon

A traveler's guide to the

HiSToRY

fascinating facts, intriguing

ALoNG The

incidents and lively legends

HiGHWaY

in Alaska's & Yukon's past

Alaska & Yukon HiSToRY ALoNG The HiGHWaY

A traveler's guide to the fascinating facts, intriguing incidents and lively legends in Alaska's & Yukon's past

Ted Stone

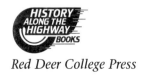

Red Deer College Press

Preface

THIS BOOK FOLLOWS TWO FAMOUS HIGHWAYS: the Alaska Highway between Dawson Creek, British Columbia, and Fairbanks, Alaska, and the Klondike Highway between Skagway, Alaska, and Dawson City, Yukon Territory. The Klondike Gold Rush and the building of the Alaska Highway transformed this great wilderness on the northwest corner of the continent in ways that will never be undone. These momentous events brought thousands of people north and changed the lives of northerners already here in profound and immeasurable ways.

Although the framework for this book reflects history along the Alaska and Klondike highways, it is not a book of local histories. I have made no attempt to write a community-by-community record of the past. Nor is this a step-by-step guide for making your way along these highways. Instead, *Alaska and Yukon History Along the Highway* is an overview of the history of Alaska and Yukon based on points of historical interest found along the highways.

Because *Alaska and Yukon History Along the Highway* is written in two sections, each following one of the highways, readers will occasionally find places where history along the two roads overlaps. Because of this, information in one section might be dealt with again in the other section. Now and again, even entries in the same section may share aspects of the same story. As much as possible, however, this kind of repetition has been avoided or kept to a minimum by making overlapping material more extensive in one entry than in another or by bringing different aspects of the same story to different entries. And although this book deals extensively with the history of the Alaska Highway and the Klondike Gold Rush, it doesn't focus on them exclusively. Occasionally it will even leave its namesake highways to follow other interesting roads that tell of other fascinating tales in the region.

Of course, no single book can include all the history that can be told about Alaska and Yukon. A writer has to choose from the thousands of stories that go into the making of any region's past. It is my hope that rather than answer all readers' questions about the history found along these highways, this book will help make any journey to Alaska and the Yukon more interesting and enjoyable. At the same time, I hope this book encourages readers to begin their own exploration of the region's fascinating history.

The reader should also note that the distances listed in *Alaska and Yukon History Along the Highway* are those actually driven by the writer, not those recorded on the mileposts found along the highways. On the Alaska Highway, the historical mileposts no longer reflect the real length of the roadway because over the years, as improvements and upgrading have been made, the length of the highway has been changed. Where steep grades have been improved, the highway has usually come away from the operation longer than it was before. Where the road has been straightened, it comes out shorter. Overall, the highway today is more than 30 miles (48 km) shorter than it was when first constructed. This, of course, makes almost all the historical mileposts along the route inaccurate.

To add to the confusion of the mileposts, Canada switched to metric measurements in the 1970s and added kilometer posts. In British Columbia these kilometer posts are based on actual driving distances from Dawson Creek, while in the Yukon the kilometer posts reflect the conversions of the old mileposts—which means the inaccuracy persists. The British Columbia–Yukon border, for instance, is at kilometer post 967.6 according to British Columbia, but at kilometer post 1009 so far as the Yukon is concerned. And when the traveler reaches the Alaska border, mileposts once again appear. But the miles are the historical miles from Dawson Creek, which, of course, are inaccurate. Sometimes, one can't help but feel the highway would have been better served had it been left in the hands of the army. With this book, forget the mile and kilometer posts, keep tabs of your actual mileage and concentrate on enjoying your travels through the North.

I must have been about 12 years old the first time I planned a trip up the Alaska Highway. While that first journey never materialized, I finally made a trip north about 10 years later, and I have gone back whenever I could ever since. Each trip is as exciting for me as the first. The North is a special place of fascinating people, spectacular wilderness and a history as exciting as anywhere on the continent. It is my hope that this book will help visitors and residents alike appreciate more fully the wonderful tales of Alaska's and Yukon's past.

Introduction
On the Trail of Alaska & Yukon History

THE KLONDIKE GOLD RUSH and the construction of the Alaska Highway were the two most extraordinary episodes in the recorded history of Alaska and the Yukon. Each in its own way brought this magnificent land on the northwestern edge of North America to the attention of southerners, and each became the impetus that brought thousands of them north.

Today, two highways, the Alaska and Klondike, make it easy for travelers to drive through the country where these historical events took place. Travelers along each road follow, literally, an historic trail. They drive over the same routes taken by the men and women who were part of those great adventures 50 and 100 years ago. Along these highways, history can embrace a traveler almost as completely as the northern wilderness itself.

Alaska and the Yukon shelter some of the last great tracks of wilderness in North America, yet human history is older here than anywhere else on the continent. Perhaps 20,000 years ago, during the last ice age, North America's first human residents traveled to this region over a land bridge from Asia. At that time, much of the landscape of Canada and the United States lay buried under towering glaciers, but large parts of today's Alaska and Yukon remained free of the ice.

The mighty Yukon River ran unimpeded through a dry ice-free oasis at the top of the continent. Because its course was never disturbed by the glaciers, the Yukon remains one of the few surviving ancient rivers of the North. Its path created a natural highway for humans, a highway where waterfalls and rapids have mostly eroded their courses over thousands of years. Long before other northern rivers like the Saskatchewan, Mackenzie, Frazer and Columbia began to grow from the melting layers of ice, the Yukon meandered freely for 2,000 miles (3,219 km) through the heart of the only settled region in North America.

When the glaciers began to retreat, bands of the continent's first human inhabitants gradually migrated south from the Yukon through an ice-free corridor opening like a funnel from today's Liard River Valley. They traveled along a break in the glaciers that stretched down the eastern side of the Rocky Mountains to the land beyond the ice in present-day Montana. Along this route, the first native Americans came to settle two continents. Much the same route would be reversed several thousand years later, when the earliest white fur traders, working for the Hudson's Bay Company, pushed their way north to the place we know today as the Yukon.

Even before the Hudson's Bay Company came to the country, however, other hunters and traders of European background had arrived on the coast of Alaska from Russia. The Danish explorer Vitus Bering, working for the Russian navy, was the first of them to see the Alaska mainland. On July 16, 1741, from his ship *St. Peter,* Bering took a sighting on a huge snow-covered peak he called Mt. St. Elias, the name honoring the saint on whose day the discovery occurred.

A few weeks after sighting Mt. St. Elias, Bering was shipwrecked on the rocky shores of a desolate island off the Alaska coast. That winter, while his crew salvaged lumber to build a boat, Bering died from the crippling effects of scurvy and malnutrition. His crew, living the entire winter off the meat of sea otters, finally completed a small vessel and in the spring of 1742 limped back to the Siberian mainland.

Their voyage might have been ignored had they not brought back sea otter pelts. Their stories of the otter's abundance on the North American coast was of immediate interest to the Russian *promyshlenniki,* ruthless bands of hunters and soldiers who roamed Siberia at that time. The *promyshlenniki* had already brought the Siberian sable population close to extinction, and when they heard about the sea otter, they began sailing for Alaska almost at once.

The *promyshlenniki* were unskilled sailors and many drowned attempting to reach the Alaska islands in unseaworthy boats. But others quickly replaced them and continued to push east to kill sea otters. Within two years they had established themselves in the western Aleutians. After that they advanced year by year, island by island, toward the Alaska mainland, slaughtering seals and the native people—the Aleuts—with equal ferocity. By 1759 the *promyshlenniki* had reached Unimak, just off the tip of the Alaska Peninsula.

As the otter population declined, however, the *promyshlenniki* began to realize that the Aleuts, whom they often slaughtered for sport, could be useful in more practical ways. The Aleuts, after all, were better hunters than the *promyshlenniki*. It made sense to use the native people to kill the increasingly hard-to-obtain otter. Gradually, the *promyshlenniki* came to depend on the Aleut hunters.

For the first 40 years of Russian settlement in Alaska, the exploitation of the new country was spontaneous and chaotic. No laws were instituted. No church was built, nor even a single European-style house. Instead, the *promyshlenniki* adopted the life of the local native people. Both the Aleut and *promyshlenniki* dressed alike. They lived in the same kinds of underground shelters. They intermarried.

Then in 1784 Russian merchant Grigon Ivanovich Shelekhov arrived with two well-equipped ships to begin the first extensive and well-organized Russian trading venture in Alaska, the Russian-American Company. Shelekhov and his wife, Natalia, established a European settlement at Three Saints Bay on the southeast shore of Kodiak Island. Within two years the colony included the village at Kodiak and more than a dozen outposts that spread all the way to Cook Inlet, 200 miles (322 km) away. But the colony remained an isolated Russian settlement without an official royal charter until after Alexander Baranov was appointed the company's manager in 1790.

Baranov ruled Alaska with an iron hand for nearly 30 years, and he developed Shelekhov's trading venture into a small but efficient empire. Soon after his arrival, Baranov began to expand his company's trading area, mostly in an effort to stave off competition from Russian poachers as well as English and American traders to the south. By the end of the century he had established Fort St. Michael at the Tlingit village of Sitka. The wealthy and warlike Tlingit tribes (Chilkoot, Chilkat and Stikines) allowed Baranov to build there only because he had purchased the site with European trade goods. Even so, when *promyshlenniki* and Aleut colonists at the Russian fort antagonized their Tlingit neighbors in 1802, the Tlingit fell on the newcomers with unchecked rage.

Most of the men of the fort were away hunting when the Tlingit attacked. But the Russians would have had little chance of resisting even if every man in the colony had been present and well armed. The Tlingit were too numerous for the tiny Russian settlement. Most of the men who remained at the fort were beheaded. The women were carried off as slaves. A few men and more than a dozen Aleut women escaped the massacre and kidnapping by hiding in the forest until they were picked up on the coast by an English pirate ship a few days later. Under the command of Henry Barber, the ship took the Russians and Aleuts back to Kodiak, where Barber ransomed them to Baranov for 10,000 rubles worth of fur pelts.

Baranov was at first helpless to retaliate against the Tlingit, but the following year Honest Joe O'Cain, a New England sea trader, arrived at Kodiak with a supply of cannons and muskets. O'Cain had been in Alaska the year before to trade supply goods to Baranov for pelts. In 1803, when he returned, Baranov invited O'Cain to form a partnership. The plan called for Baranov to lend Aleut hunters to the New England sea captain to take to the coast of California along with a Russian overseer. Here, the Aleut would hunt sea otters for O'Cain. In exchange, Baranov was to receive half of whatever pelts his hunters killed, plus the supply of muskets and cannons he needed to use against the Tlingit.

Too late in the season to do anything about the Indians at Sitka that year, Baranov set out the following spring with 120 *promyshlenniki* and 800 Aleuts in 4 small ships and 400 Aleut kayaks. By the time the armada, outfitted with O'Cain's cannons and muskets, reached Sitka, it had been joined by the frigate *Neva*, the first Russian fighting ship to sail on the Pacific.

Soon the *Neva*'s cannons, and those on Baranov's four smaller ships, were turned on the Tlingit village. They shelled Sitka for several days before Baranov led his Aleut forces ashore. Even after the terrible days of shelling, the Tlingit were able to quickly drive Baranov's forces back to the sea. Immediately afterward, shelling from the cannons started again. Only after several more days did the Tlingit finally abandon their village, allowing Baranov to lead his men into the town.

With the Tlingit out of the way, Baranov built a new fort. This time he moved quickly to make the post strong enough to resist any Tlingit retaliation. As part of the process, he moved to Sitka himself. He made his new fort the administrative center for the Russian-American Company in Alaska and named his new capital New Archangel, although the name Sitka continued to be used.

The Russian-American Company prospered at the new location. Tens of thousands of pelts per year flowed to the company, many coming from as far away as California through Baranov's partnership with O'Cain. Sitka became a regular stop on the Pacific trade route for American and English ships. Baranov even sent an expeditionary force to California, where he established a Russian fort and agricultural colony 25 miles (40 km) north of the Spanish at San Francisco.

In 1817 Baranov retired to Russia, but the Russian-American Company continued for another 50 years. Over this time, 13 governors, including a Russian prince, came and left Alaska with their wives and aristocratic aides. Life in the colony became progressively more elegant, even as the importance of the fur trade that sustained it declined. Relations with the Tlingit gradually improved, although the cannons that lined the stockade walls of New Archangel always pointed toward the native village of Sitka.

While the Russians traded for sea otter pelts along the Alaska coast, English and Canadian fur traders moved steadily west and northwest across the top of the continent toward the Yukon. Alexander Mackenzie, working for the North West Company, was the first European to note the existence of the Yukon River. In 1789, while Mackenzie followed the river that today bears his name, Indians told him of a large river over the mountains to the west that flowed into another ocean. Mackenzie recorded what he learned of this river in his journal. Later, when the journal was published and then translated into Russian, a Russian search for the river began in Alaska.

In 1840 Robert Campbell became the first Hudson's Bay Company trader to arrive on the Yukon watershed when he crossed the continental divide from the Liard and Frances rivers to the Pelly. Although the Russians had discovered the lower reaches of the Yukon River by this time, they had not penetrated very far upstream into the Alaska interior. Campbell opened the first trading post on the upper Yukon at Fort Selkirk in 1848.

About the same time, another Hudson's Bay Company trading post, Fort Yukon, was established downstream at the mouth of the Porcupine, inside present-day Alaska. Traders arrived at Fort Yukon from the north, however, coming via Fort McPherson, on the Mackenzie delta, and, after crossing the mountain divide, the Porcupine River. For three years none of the Hudson's Bay men knew for sure if the two new posts were on the same river. Only when Robert Campbell traveled downstream to Fort Yukon from Fort Selkirk in 1851 was there proof that the two trading posts were on the same waterway.

Campbell's Fort Selkirk was in a traditional Chilkat trading area. When he first arrived, the Chilkat—a northern coastal branch of the Tlingit—tolerated the new English trader. His goods, after all, were inferior and higher priced than the ones the Chilkat brought to the interior Indians from their home on the coast. Once Campbell discovered that his river was the same as Fort Yukon's, however, he immediately began getting goods and supplies from the north instead of the more dangerous and expensive route up the Liard from the south. With this simple change Hudson's Bay trade goods suddenly became competitive with the Chilkat's—a development that so angered them, they attacked and destroyed Fort Selkirk. Campbell was sent scurrying back to Montreal, and Fort Yukon was left as the only Hudson's Bay post on the upper river.

But Fort Yukon wasn't even in British territory. By treaty, Russian America began at the 141st Meridian. Fort Yukon was well west of that line, and the Hudson's Bay Company knew it. The only Russian posts on the river were far downstream, however, and the English company gambled that the Russians would stay there. It was a gamble that paid off. Not until 25 years later, after the Russian sale of Alaska to the United States, did anyone challenge the position of the Hudson's Bay Company on the Yukon.

The Americans negotiated the purchase of Alaska in March 1867 during a secret meeting in the middle of the night in Washington, D.C. But the sale, the second largest real estate transaction in American history, should have come as no surprise to anyone. Moscow had looked on the cost of administering Russia's American colony as a burden for some time. Only the fear that the territory would be taken over by the English and the knowledge that the Americans might be willing to buy it kept the imperial government in the North American colonial picture.

Secretary of State William H. Seward was indeed anxious to purchase Alaska. So anxious, in fact, that he spent $2–3 million more than the Russians would have been willing to sell it for. As it was, Seward's price of $7.2 million was still a bargain, only a little over two cents an acre (.5 ha)—for 586,000 square miles (1,517,623 sq km) of territory.

Still, the purchase was ridiculed by many in Congress and in the press. Congressman Benjamin F. Butler of Massachusetts said that while he didn't mind spending the money to buy Russia's friendship, he thought it was a shame to have to take Alaska as part of the bargain. Approval of the treaty came hard in the United States Senate. Later, Congress almost failed to provide the funds to complete the purchase. Even then it took more than a generation before most Americans began to appreciate Alaska's significance.

A few, though, saw potential opportunities in the North. Even before Congress voted funds to complete the purchase in 1868, several hundred Americans had already made their way north. At the time, there were about 30,000 indigenous people scattered throughout the future state (about half the number who had lived there when the Russians first arrived) as well as a few Russian nationals, who stayed on after the transfer of territory, and several thousand mixed-blood people.

After reluctantly approving the purchase, Congress refused in the next few years to spend anything more on Alaska than the minimum required for military administration of the new possession. Although residents petitioned the government for territorial status in order to establish some form of legal government, their calls were ignored. Commercial activity began to decline after an initial flurry of transactions. At Sitka, a Russian oasis of civilization, life soon suffered from American neglect. By 1870 most of Alaska's first American residents had turned around and gone home.

There were a few economic exceptions to the general malaise that overtook the new territory. Seal hunting became the first and most obvious. Not only did the seal harvest continue after the American takeover, but prices for pelts increased substantially. When the Russian-American Company abandoned Alaska in 1867, the American Hayward M. Hutchinson, along with several San Francisco partners, bought all the Alaskan assets of the old Russian fur company. These included steamers, sailing ships, wharves and even furs left behind in warehouses at Sitka, Kodiak, Unalaska and the Pribilof Islands.

In 1868 the new company incorporated itself as the Alaska Commercial Company. Its first order of business was to lobby the United States Congress for laws under which it could operate. Ideally, it wanted the same kind of monopoly the Russian company had enjoyed. The new company was for the most part successful. In 1870 Congress established a protected federal reserve on the Pribilof Islands breeding grounds. It allowed seal hunting but limited the size of the harvest. In addition, the government leased to the highest bidder the exclusive right to hunt the fur seals.

The highest bidder, of course, turned out to be the Alaska Commercial Company. Over the next 25 years, the seal harvest made millions of dollars for the company's owners and also returned to the United States government, in royalties, more than the original purchase price for all Alaska. The conservation measures written into the law also established some protection for the seal population. The weak point in legislated resource protection was the United States' lack of jurisdiction in international waters. Canadian hunters continued to take seals in waters outside the U.S. limits, which left seals as vulnerable to overhunting as they would have been with no prohibitions. Finally, in 1911, a treaty was negotiated that prohibited the hunting of seals anywhere but on land, but by then much of the seal population had been destroyed.

While the Alaska Commercial Company proved that money could still be made in furs, economic activity in the rest of Alaska continued to stagnate. In 1877 even the army pulled out, leaving only a handful of government officials in all Alaska. The situation got so bad that in 1879, when the Tlingit again threatened Sitka, residents there, fearing no help from their own government, sent a request for aid to the British man-o'-war HMS *Ospry* out of Victoria, British Columbia.

The British naval ship hurried north, arriving at Sitka on March 1. Immediately, the British ship trained its guns on the Tlingit village. For over a month the British waited until the U.S. Navy gunboat *Alaska* finally arrived from San Francisco. Even with this humiliation the United States government continued to ignore Alaska until 1884. Then Congress passed the Organic Act of Alaska, a bill that placed the region under the civil and criminal laws of Oregon Territory. This allowed Alaska to establish its first legitimate government with a governor and court system. The first government allocation for the education of children was also established.

Meanwhile, a second front of economic activity began to make headway. Ever since the California Gold Rush of 1849, prospectors had been crisscrossing the American and Canadian West looking for new bonanzas. Starting in Colorado, gold rush followed gold rush to Montana, Idaho and British Columbia. For those who took the time to look—and many did—there was a pattern to the strikes that suggested the next logical discovery would come in the far north in Alaska and along the Yukon River in Canada.

Three of the Yukon's earliest prospectors—Jack McQuesten, Arthur Harper and Al Mayo—arrived on the river in the early 1870s. They came north from Canada's Peace River country. Mayo and McQuesten had already been friends for a number of years, and they met Harper on their way north. They came into the country on the old Hudson's Bay route down the Porcupine River after crossing the divide from the Mackenzie to Fort Yukon. At the time there were probably no more than half a dozen prospectors strung out over the entire 2,000-mile course of the river.

McQuesten built a trading post called Fort Reliance for the Alaska Commercial Company six miles below the mouth of the Klondike River in 1873. For the next 25 years the three men operated trading posts in partnership, individually and as independent traders for the Alaska Commercial Company. They also prospected when they could and encouraged more miners to come into the area whenever the opportunity presented itself.

In 1882 a promising strike was made on the Fortymile River (40 miles below Fort Reliance). Then three years later, gold discoveries on the Stewart River brought on the first significant influx of prospectors from outside the Yukon Valley. This prompted Mayo, McQuesten and Harper to open a new post on the Stewart. Soon, though, a new and richer strike on the Fortymile sent miners hurrying back downstream.

By the following spring hundreds of miners had pushed into the Yukon Valley from southeastern Alaska. The town of Fortymile lay on the Canadian side of the border at the river's mouth on the Yukon. But the international boundary was, for all intents and purposes, nonexistent. Although Fortymile was in Canada, most of the gold claims were upstream on the Alaska side of the boundary. But no customs duties were collected. No laws were enforced—except for those passed at miners' meetings, the extralegal committees that in the absence of civil authority had become a fixture in mining camps all over the West. Only when the North-West Mounted Police arrived nearly a decade later would either national government exert any official influence in the upper Yukon Valley. Only then would a border between the two countries have any practical meaning for the miners who lived along the river.

The town of Fortymile during the spring flood of 1896.

Inspector Charles Constantine with North-West Mounted Police at Fortymile in 1896.

Although the Fortymile strike sparked the first large gold rush in the Yukon Valley, it was not the first big gold discovery in Alaska. That came in 1880 when two American ne'er-do-wells, Richard Harris and Joseph Juneau, staked claims in the Panhandle region and laid out a townsite that would, one day, become Alaska's capital. Harris and Juneau had arrived at Sitka the previous year, looking for work and still owing the price of their passage north.

Grubstaked in Sitka by George Pilz, the pair set out in a small boat with three months' provisions to search for gold along the fjords and islands of the Alaska Panhandle. Tired of prospecting after only a couple of weeks, the two men put in at an Auk Indian village. Here, they traded provisions for liquor and women until little was left of their grubstake except their rifle and the clothes on their backs. Even their boat had drifted away, so they had to trade the rifle to the Indians in exchange for a ride back to Sitka.

On the return trip, Harris and Juneau promised Auk Chief Cowee 100 blankets if he could show them any gold-producing streams. Cowee took them to the mouth of a small stream at the head of Gastineau Channel. The banks of the creek were thick with brush, so Harris and Juneau, still hung over from their weeks spent drinking *hoochinoo*—the Indian's homemade liquor—ignored Cowee's pleas to follow him upstream.

Cowee protested all the way back to Sitka. Once there, the Indian took samples of gold he'd taken from the creek to George Pilz, explaining that there was much more gold farther up the creek. Pilz was excited about the find and wanted to send someone to stake claims. The trouble was that Harris and Juneau were the only unemployed men in Sitka. It was already late in the year, so Pilz decided to gamble. He sent Harris and Juneau back to the Gastineau Channel with Cowee and several other Auks. This time, the pair staked claims as well as a townsite of 160 acres on the side of Gastineau Channel.

Cowee's gold discovery sparked the first major Alaska gold rush, and many of the early miners became wealthy in the ventures that followed. A single claim on nearby Douglas Island, bought by the Californian John Treadwell, yielded nearly $70 million. The town that Juneau and Harris surveyed was originally called Harrisburg, but in 1881 miners of the district, angry that Harris had staked multiple claims contrary to custom, renamed the new mining town Juneau.

As for Harris, he took out about $75,000 in gold from his claims but soon squandered it. He died in 1907 in an Oregon sanitarium. Juneau made about $18,000 from his claim and was broke again within two years. He died in Dawson City in 1899. Miners there took up a collection to have his body returned to Juneau, where he had once asked to be buried. Cowee was given his 100 blankets.

Stampeders climb the Chilkoot Pass during the winter of 1897-98.

One of the major effects of the Juneau Gold Rush was that it brought more prospectors to Alaska. Miners came from Colorado, Idaho and the Cassiar District of British Columbia. Afterward, they prospected up and down the Alaska Panhandle. When word reached them of the new strikes in the Yukon Valley, on the Stewart and Fortymile rivers, many of them headed over the Chilkoot Pass, creating the first significant influx of people to the Yukon and Alaska interior.

By the 1890s an estimated 2,500 people lived along the Yukon River. The town of Fortymile boasted a variety of businesses, including stores, saloons and even a barber. In 1895 the North-West Mounted Police arrived to establish their first post in the Yukon. The stage was now set for the Klondike Gold Rush of 1897–98.

On August 17, 1896, George Carmack and two Yukon Indians, Skookum Jim and Tagish Charlie discovered gold on a creek that would soon be known as Bonanza. It was too late in the season for word to reach the outside world before freeze-up, but the following July, when the first steamships carrying Yukon miners docked at San Francisco and Seattle, the last great gold rush of the 19th century got underway. Before it had run its course, the Klondike Stampede had brought 100,000 people north to Alaska and the Yukon. In the process both places were changed forever.

North-West Mounted Police post at Fortymile in 1896.

The Klondike was never North America's richest gold discovery, but it did produce some of the most spectacular individual claims. It also sparked one of the biggest and most difficult mass migrations of gold seekers in the continent's history. Established in 1896, Dawson City, the capital of the Klondike, saw as many as 40,000 people arrive in town between 1897 and 1899. For a short time Dawson, only 150 miles south of the Arctic Circle, was the largest city west of Chicago and north of Seattle. Although the town survived as a gold-mining region even after the gold rush, the majority of its new inhabitants moved on soon after arriving. Many of the stampeders left town without even looking for gold.

For those more serious about prospecting, there would soon be other gold rushes. Even in 1898 prospectors were already fanning out to other points along the Yukon, up the Stewart and Pelly rivers, across the Chilkoot Pass to the Atlin region of British Columbia, back to Circle City in the Yukon—all in search of an elusive gold-producing stream that would mark their place in history and make them rich overnight.

Dawson City at the turn of the century.

In 1899 Dawson saw a mass exodus of people bound for the new diggings at Nome. By 1903 a new gold strike on the Chena River in the Tanana District had brought miners back to the Alaska interior. The town of Fairbanks was to become, in the words of new Alaska judge James Wickersham, an American Dawson City. Gold, while responsible for only a small part of the wealth of Alaska and the Yukon, had served to populate the two territories.

Other explorers had helped open the territory, but it was the miners who brought the modern world north. Fairbanks was said to be the first modern gold rush town. A telegraph and road from Valdez were established early. Judge Wickersham's court meant there was no need for miners' meetings to establish law and order. The Northern Commercial Company supplied the community with electricity. And the gold of the area was buried somewhat deeper than in previous gold rush sites, so machinery for its extraction came to the Chena early. This created an extended boom for Fairbanks, one that lasted a decade instead of the more typical boom-and-bust gold rush economies, which lasted anywhere from a few weeks or months to two or three years.

With the basic settlement of Alaska and the Yukon complete by the early years of the century, the economies of both territories stabilized around resource industries. These were, with few exceptions, controlled by large companies and syndicates. When World War II began, the construction of the Alaska Highway once again brought people and money north. The highway, built under military necessity, was a marvel of engineering and speedy construction. As a military road, however, the Alaska Highway's significance declined almost as fast as it was built.

For the people of Alaska and the Yukon, the highway changed the North in profound ways. It opened the country literally and psychologically. Alaska and Yukon were no longer cut off from the rest of North America. Many of the workers who came north during the war stayed. After the war, the highway brought tourists and new residents. After 1960, when Alaska became a state, even more Americans headed north to the country's last frontier. To a lesser extent, the same thing happened on the Canadian side of the boundary.

Today, Alaska and the Yukon—possessing some of the largest and most spectacular wilderness areas left on the continent—play an integral part in North American life. Roads, once a rarity in the North, now crisscross Alaska and the Yukon, from the southern tip of the Alaska Panhandle all the way to the Arctic Ocean. The Alaska and Klondike highways take visitors through spectacular mountain vistas, unspoiled wilderness and an incredibly rich and interesting history.

Chapter 1

The Klondike Trail

Skagway to Dawson City

A RRIVING AT THE PORT OF SKAGWAY TODAY, visitors discover a place that looks much the way it did 100 years ago at the height of the Klondike Gold Rush. Eagles still soar above the water of Lynn Canal. Clouds still cling to the sides of the snow-covered Coast Mountains. At the head of the inlet, at the old townsite of Dyea, the tidal flats still stretch far out to the sea at low tide.

Skagway's Main Street in 1898.

In Skagway board sidewalks and false-fronted stores with painted names like The Red Onion Saloon, Lynch & Kennedy's Dry Goods and Keller's Trading Company lend the town an appropriate 1890s frontier atmosphere. In Skagway you can still find Jeff Smith's Parlor (once owned by the town's legendary gangster Soapy Smith) or take a ride on the famous White Pass & Yukon Route railway or even outfit yourself for a hike over the Chilkoot Pass. In Skagway, just as in Dawson City 400 miles (644 km) to the north, a compelling gold rush legacy lingers, bringing the Klondike Stampede to life across a century of time.

It all started on August 17, 1896. That's when three Klondike prospectors—Skookum Jim, Tagish Charlie and George Carmack —discovered a rich deposit of placer gold on Rabbit Creek, a tributary of the Klondike River. The three men staked their claims and renamed the creek Bonanza. While Skookum Jim watched over their claim, Carmack and Tagish Charlie headed for the mining town of Fortymile, 50 miles (81 km) downstream on the Yukon River. As they traveled, they told everyone they met along the way of their great find.

Some of the old-timers at Fortymile ignored the news, dismissing George Carmack as a notorious liar and claiming the conditions on the Klondike weren't right for a major gold strike. Most sourdoughs, though, were ready to take a chance on the news. In a short time miners from up and down the river found themselves scrambling to get to the Klondike. Within a few weeks most of the claims close to the discovery had already been staked.

It took until January for dependable news of the Klondike strike to reach Circle City in Alaska, but when it did, the town virtually emptied within 24 hours. This left Circle, which had only recently become Alaska's largest Yukon River community, with only two residents. Even so, by the time Circle City miners arrived upriver at the mouth of the Klondike, it was too late for most of them to get in on any of the rich claims on Bonanza or Eldorado creeks.

Despite this flurry of activity in the Klondike, which resulted in almost every claim worth owning being taken by Yukon miners, the real Klondike Stampede did not start until the following summer in July 1897. There was hardly a more isolated spot on the North American continent than the upper Yukon River Valley, so nothing but rumors of the gold strike filtered south for nearly 11 months. When the first steamships carrying gold and miners from the Yukon arrived in San Francisco and Seattle, however, news of the rich discovery in the Klondike soon swept the continent. "A Ton of Gold," one headline proclaimed. "Millions Still In The Ground," said another. "Gold, Gold, Gold," said a third.

In 1897 North Americans were ready for a bout of dizziness and frenzy of the magnitude that tales of Klondike gold set off. For thousands life in the Gay Nineties had been decidedly unblissful. The world lingered in a drawn-out economic depression. The earning power of working people decreased, while stories about families of great wealth—like the Rockefellers, Vanderbilts and other barons of the new industrial age—captivated the popular imagination. The shortage of gold to back currency prompted presidential candidate William Jennings Bryan to declare that humanity should not be "crucified on a cross of gold." But for many, gold seemed the surest and quickest cure to their economic problems.

The nineties were also a time of sensationalist journalism, and when the ships came in from Alaska laden with gold, there was no more sensational story around than the Klondike miners seen staggering down gangplanks, swaying under their heavy packs and suitcases loaded with gold dust and nuggets. For several months, until the Spanish-American War brought a new diversion, newspapers mined news from the Yukon for every ounce they could get.

A miner pays with gold dust at a Dawson City store.

Almost as soon as the first ship from Alaska carrying Yukon miners arrived in San Francisco, people started lining up at shipping company ticket windows in cities all along the West Coast. People bought passage on any vessel going north that would float, including some of questionable seaworthiness. Several ships, in fact, did sink, and only blind luck kept others afloat. But people still fought for tickets on any ship bound for the Yukon.

One of the earliest stampeders to make money on the Klondike Gold Rush did so without leaving Seattle. He bought a ticket to Alaska for $150, and a few days later he sold it for $1,500. All of a sudden, thousands upon thousands of people were ready to give up everything they had for a chance to go to the Klondike. Those who couldn't go joined syndicates and raised enough money to send one or two of their members. The fact that most of them had no idea where the Klondike might be located deterred none.

Stampeders on their way to Dawson in 1898.

They came from all over North America and the world. Those with enough money bought passage to St. Michael on the Bering Sea. At this isolated outpost they boarded Yukon River steamers that carried them the still formidable 1,700 additional miles (2,736 km) to Dawson City. A few misguided souls rode the railroads north as far as the end of steel at Edmonton, Alberta. From there, stampeders struck cross-country, trying to follow the old Hudson's Bay Company fur trails to the Yukon. Or they traveled down the Athabasca and Mackenzie rivers into the high Arctic, planning to cross over the Richardson Mountains to other rivers leading directly to the gold fields. The lucky ones gave up on these routes early in the journey and returned home.

Goats pull sled and supplies to the Klondike in 1898.

Cities up and down the West Coast did a brisk business during the Klondike Stampede by supplying men and women heading for Dawson City. Thomas Dunn & Company was a prominent Vancouver outfitter.

Still other gold seekers followed a variety of so-called all-Canadian routes to the Klondike. Some even tried to cross the Malaspina Glacier on an all-American route. A few went over the Dalton Trail from Haines Mission. But of the 200,000 or so gold seekers who actually set out for the Yukon, the vast majority who made it to Dawson City came north from Seattle, San Francisco, Victoria or one of the other West Coast cities where they could board ocean steamers to take them up the Inside Passage to the gold rush boomtowns of Dyea and Skagway.

Both towns had sprouted side by side almost overnight in July 1897. Each was at the head of a trail leading inland to the headwaters of the Yukon River. When the Klondike Gold Rush began, stampeders crossed the mountains over the White Pass from Skagway or over the Chilkoot from Skagway's coastal neighbor, Dyea. Many who had come north to go to the Yukon took one look at the snow-capped barriers towering above the towns and booked passage on the next steamship going south.

But approximately 40,000 others, pushed on over one or the other of the mountain passes, then down the Yukon River to the gold fields of the Klondike.

Most stampeders spent several months getting to the Klondike. Today, travelers can drive the Klondike Highway from Skagway to Dawson City at the mouth of the Klondike River— making stops along the way—in the course of a day.

Stampeders with stacked supplies on the beach at Dyea in 1897.

Gold Rush Stampeders Arrive at Skagway
Alaska State Ferry Terminal, Skagway Waterfront, Skagway

These days, thousands of visitors on the cruise ships that ply the waters of the Inside Passage or aboard Alaska State Ferries come to Skagway every summer. In numbers, today's visitors can sometimes rival the influx of people that occurred during the heady days of the gold rush. But the orderly crowds of tourists strolling from store to store along Skagway's busy streets today don't create anything like the chaos that befell the town when the crowds came in 1897.

The first steamship load of stampeders stormed ashore on July 26 of that year, and the quiet beaches at the head of Lynn Canal have never been the same since. By the first of August, the bay was alive with all manner of boats and wagons. The shallow water of the canal forced steamships to anchor as much as a mile from shore, while passengers and their cargoes were ferried to shore in scows, lighters and even canoes.

Many of the thousands of stampeders who arrived brought horses and dogs north with them, and both were sometimes dumped into the sea to swim ashore. The horses, which could be used on the trails, brought good prices in Skagway, but the dogs—brought north under the stampeders' vague and mistaken notions about Eskimo dogs used to pull sleighs—were southern pets of no practical value in the North. Most were immediately abandoned, adding to the general mayhem of Skagway streets.

The waterfront was a tumult of people, canvas tents, crated goods, campfires, sacks of flour, sides of bacon, wild-eyed horses and stray dogs. Stampeders often lost their supplies in the piles of unloaded cargo that sprawled in giant stacks across the beaches. Sometimes goods unloaded below the high tide mark weren't moved to higher ground fast enough, leaving food, clothes, ammunition and camping gear submerged in salt water when the tide waters returned.

Behind the waterfront, the town of Skagway emerged as the stampeders arrived. False-fronted hotels, restaurants, dance halls and gambling joints rose where the recently vanquished forest had stood only weeks before. Saloons, which often started out in tents before moving indoors, sprang up all over town, though whiskey and other spirituous liquors had been supposedly outlawed. An assortment of enterprises in canvas tents and slapped-together board shacks seemed to come and go with the tides. "Skagway," said Sam Steele, the superintendent of the North-West Mounted Police, "was little better than hell on earth."

Soapy Smith Runs Skagway
Broadway Avenue, Skagway

Jefferson Randolph "Soapy" Smith arrived in Skagway in the late summer or early autumn of 1897 with five followers in tow. At the time, the only money Smith had in his pocket he'd borrowed from one of his companions. Within three months Smith had taken control of the new boomtown of Skagway, reaping thousands of dollars a week through several illicit businesses and small-time swindling operations.

Smith was a Georgian who presented himself erroneously as the scion of a prominent Southern family. The nickname came from one of Soapy's favorite street-corner bunco games back in the mining camps of Colorado. For $5, Smith would offer passersby their choice of several bars of soap, a few of which supposedly had $20- and $50-bills tucked inside their wrappers. Soapy's accomplices bought the soap with the money wrapped inside and always made a big show of their winnings. The suckers on the street, though, were never able to buy anything but soap.

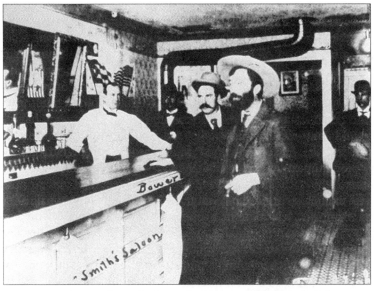

Soapy Smith stands at the bar of a Skagway saloon on July 4, 1898. He was shot five days later by Frank Reid.

Soapy swindled the miners of Colorado with his soap game and other similar scams for years. By the time the Klondike Gold Rush started, however, life had become precariously warm for the increasingly well-known bunco man of Leadville and Denver. Smith decided to take his operations north. He planned to set himself up as a leading upright citizen of the new community of Skagway, then milk the town for every cent he could.

Soapy got his start in Skagway operating out of Clancy's

Saloon but soon opened his own place, Jeff Smith's Parlor, on Holly Street (today's 6th Avenue). From this small drinking establishment, eatery and game room he proceeded to organize an array of illicit businesses and swindle joints, all designed to siphon as much money as possible from the transient population of Skagway. Soapy tried to make sure his men left permanent residents alone so as not to stir up any unnecessary trouble.

It was said that Soapy's network of spies reached as far south as Seattle. These men would send him word when wealthy passengers left for Skagway. Usually, a member of Soapy's gang would then be waiting at the docks to steer the unsuspecting travelers to whichever of Soapy's scam joints seemed most appropriate.

Soapy had dozens of novel ways to relieve a man of his money. His telegraph office showed particular genius. There was, of course, no telegraph line to Skagway, but this was no impediment to Soapy Smith. He had his men open an office anyway on one of Skagway's side streets. For the price of five dollars a man could send a telegram anywhere in the world. Thousands paid to send word to their families that they were leaving town for the mountain passes and the Klondike. Not content with making only five dollars off a sucker, Smith usually arranged for an appropriately worded return message to arrive—collect, of course—just before the man left town.

Soapy's fast-growing gang included men like the "Reverend" Charles Bowers, who used his pious kind-hearted manner to steer argonauts with money to one or another of Soapy's gyp joints. Other gang members included those whose apparent benevolence was equal to that of Bowers', while still others were nothing more than common pickpockets, muggers, sneak thieves and thugs. The standard procedure for all their enterprises called for Soapy Smith to receive 50 percent of the take.

Members of Soapy's gang also opened a travel agency that gave out free information and sold maps of the route to the gold fields for the cut-rate price of a dollar. This allowed members of the gang to get a quick look inside every map purchaser's wallet. When a wallet seemed large enough to bother about, one of the gang stationed nearby would grab the money and run. Other gang members would make a pretense of chasing after the man but would only block the victim from the doorway long enough for their fellow gang member to escape.

Sometimes, when victims of Smith's crimes were left penniless, unable to go on to the gold fields or return home, Smith would come forward as a public benefactor, anxious to help a poor man return to his family back in the States and pay for his ticket home. This, of course, put the man in no position to stir up public resentment against Soapy. Another way to do the same thing, of course, was to have the man shot, which also sometimes happened.

Smith did organize legitimate civic charities in early Skagway. Within a few weeks of his arrival, Smith began to publicly support local widows whose husbands had been killed on the trail, as well as other needy people in town. He had accounts with several merchants that he used exclusively for charitable items. Sometimes these accounts amounted to several hundred dollars a week.

Of course, many of those in need were in that position because of the actions of Smith's gang of desperadoes, but Smith's image remained that of public benefactor. He took in six of the town's stray dogs, for instance, and urged other residents to do the same. Once, under the guise of raising money to build a church, Soapy toured the saloons until he had collected several thousand dollars, which he gave to a newly arrived preacher in a self-aggrandizing public ceremony. That very night, however, Smith ordered the poor parson robbed of every cent. Another time, Smith actually donated money to help build Skagway's first church.

Smith's eloquence and charm made him a formidable character in the townspeople's eyes. Once, when a Skagway mob was searching the town, intending to hang a friend of Soapy's who had murdered two men, including the deputy marshall, Soapy quelled the crowd by speaking out against mob action and for the rule of law. Dramatically, he declared that mobs and lynching had no place in Skagway, and anyone attempting to hang the murderer without a fair trial would have to shoot Soapy Smith, too. His argument was so persuasive that the crowd backed down. Smith, whose gambling friends had been hiding the murderer, then got the man to give himself up. Under the guise of sending him to Juneau and justice, Soapy had the murderer spirited off to Sitka and freedom. Meanwhile, Smith enhanced his reputation as an upright citizen even further by starting a drive to raise money for the widows and children of the murder victims.

No one knows how much money Smith and his men stole or how many people who took offense at his behavior were murdered. But gradually resentment began to build among Skagway's honest citizens. A newly formed vigilante committee issued warnings but took no real action for weeks, partly because Soapy Smith had so many people on his payroll that nobody knew for sure who might be one of his spies. Resentment continued to build until early in July 1898 Smith was killed in a shoot-out with Frank Reid, Skagway's town surveyor. Reid, whom Smith had managed to shoot in the groin, died from his wound twelve days later.

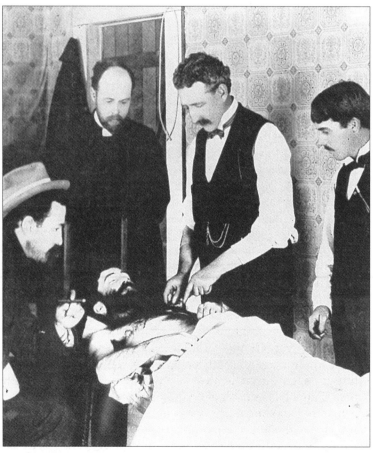

A Skagway doctor performs an autopsy on crime boss Soapy Smith in 1898.

Newcomers Steal Captain Moore's Skagway
Moore Cabin and Homestead, Broadway Avenue, Skagway

Captain Billy Moore was 75 years old when the Klondike Gold Rush began. He had been in Alaska for more than 10 years. Over the course of his life, which had taken him from gold stampede to gold stampede all across North and South America, Moore had made and lost several fortunes. He'd started with the California Gold Rush in 1849 and went broke for the last time in the Cassiar District in northern British Columbia. The Cassiar bankruptcy came about when the gold rush there ended before Moore had extracted enough profits to pay for several steamboats he'd brought in to supply miners.

In 1887 Moore headed for the Yukon to try for gold one more time. His first undertaking was as a member of a Canadian government surveying team led by William Ogilvie. Moore had already heard about a mysterious mountain pass near the Chilkoot, rarely used by the Tlingit. According to the story, the pass was low enough for horse travel. Ogilvie had also heard of the pass, and the two men decided that while Ogilvie and the rest of the survey party, including their Tlingit packers, went over the Chilkoot Trail, Moore would try to cross the mountains over the other pass.

Moore's guide over the new pass was a Tagish Indian named Skookum Jim, who nine years later became one of the co-discoverers of gold in the Klondike. Skookum Jim agreed to show Moore the way in exchange for the promise that Moore would not let Jim's Tlingit neighbors know anything about what he had done. The Tlingit had traditionally controlled all access to the mountain passes, but they now allowed more or less free access to the Chilkoot because they could make money there as packers for the white miners. The Tagish, on the other hand, still faced many restrictions in Tlingit land. Skookum Jim knew the Tlingit would be particularly angry at any Tagish who showed a white man an alternate route to the interior, especially one where Tlingit packers might be unnecessary.

It took Skookum Jim several days to lead Moore over the pass, climbing along precipitous hillsides and rocky canyons, scrambling over downed trees and through boggy river bottoms. The trail turned out to be longer than the Chilkoot by about 10 miles (16 km), but not nearly as steep and certainly better suited for horses if it were cleaned up. A wagon road could be built and perhaps, thought Moore, even a railroad. When Moore and Skookum Jim finally rejoined the survey party at Lake Bennett, Ogilvie, too, was pleased to learn about the pass. He named it after his boss, Thomas White, the Canadian minister of the interior at the time.

As for Captain Moore, the more he thought about the White Pass and its potential as a route to the Yukon River the more excited he became. After completing his contract with the Canadian government, he hurried back to Skagway Bay. In October he filed for 160 acres (65 ha) of land at the head of the pass and began building a cabin. Moore was already convinced that a large gold strike would be made in the Yukon. When the discovery came, he felt sure his new pass would be the main highway to the gold fields.

Moore predicted that a town would be born on his new land on Skagway Bay, that steamboats would ply the waters of the upper Yukon and even that a railroad would be built over the mountains to connect Yukon River traffic with Skagway. He constructed a wharf on the waterfront, began improving the trail over the White Pass, had his property surveyed and built a sawmill—all in anticipation of a town he would call Mooresville.

It took a decade, but events suddenly began to unfold just as Moore had predicted. Only the extent of the new gold rush surprised him. The stampeders began streaming in on July 29, 1897, and before Moore could do anything about it, men began cutting trees to build cabins, clearing land to make space for the tons of supplies arriving daily from the south and resurveying his townsite. They even changed the name of the new town from Mooresville to Skagway, the traditional name of the river and bay next to which the town grew up.

Thousands of stampeders poured ashore. Many of them, intent on getting rich without even going to the gold fields, began staking lots and dividing up Moore's land to take advantage of other stampeders. Soon the townsite had become such a jumble of stakes and tents that a committee was formed to arrange for a formal survey of the town. Ignoring Captain Moore's claims of ownership, local bartender and surveyor Frank Reid was appointed to lay out streets with 50 x 100' (15- x 30-M) lots. The following summer Reid would be killed in a gun battle with the new town's infamous crime boss, Soapy Smith.

The claim jumpers taking over Moore's property soon developed a thriving real estate trade. When all the lots in the new town had been sold or claimed, prices began to rise precipitously. Some who had sold lots to miners passing through town on their way to the gold fields even started reselling the same lots. No one paid attention to the protestations of Captain Billy Moore in the real estate frenzy. In fact, the new town survey placed one of Moore's buildings squarely in the middle of the new Main Street. When Moore refused to move it, the claim jumpers hauled it off to the waterfront.

Being a law-abiding man—at least after he failed to beat the mob away from his building with a crowbar—Moore took his case to court. But lawyers and courts of law took a long time, even at the end of the last century. When Moore won his case four years later, the gold rush was over and the days of inflated real estate prices in Skagway had passed. Moore's settlement of 25 percent of the currently assessed value of his old property didn't amount to anything like the sum he would have made had he been able to sell his lots during the height of the Klondike Stampede.

But it was still a tidy profit. Besides, Captain Billy Moore hadn't fared badly during the gold rush. His sawmill had supplied much of the lumber from which the new town of Skagway had been built. And he sold his wharf to the builders of the White Pass & Yukon Route railway for an estimated $150,000. Moore left Skagway and built a new house in Victoria, British Columbia, where he retired a moderately wealthy man.

Harriet Pullen Runs Best Hotel in Skagway
Pullen House Site Interpretive Signs, Spring Street, Skagway

While Captain Moore was trying to get his land back and Soapy Smith and his gang were busy taking over the seedy side of Skagway, other residents of the new town were trying to make an honest life. Prominent among them was Harriet Pullen, who arrived about the same time Soapy did in the late summer of 1897.

Pullen, a widow with four children, had been forced from a bankrupt farm back in Washington State. But Pullen proved to be the epitome of resilience, industry and ingenuity. When she got off the steamer *Rosalie* in Skagway, she had seven dollars in her pocket, which she used to open a restaurant. The tent where she set up business was so small that she couldn't stand upright to work. Undeterred she pounded pie tins out of old tin cans, bought some dried apples and began baking pies.

Before long she was able to move to a log cabin and send for her three young sons back in Washington, leaving her youngest child, a daughter, with relatives for the time being. She also had her sons bring along the seven horses she still owned. Pullen had seen packers earning as much as $25 a day taking supplies over the White Pass and decided she could do the same. After her horses arrived, Pullen freighted outfits over the White Pass during the day and continued to run her restaurant at night. The White Pass was notoriously hard on horses, killing several hundred during the gold rush, but Pullen was an excellent horsewoman. Only one of her animals suffered even a minor injury during her time on the trail.

After the construction of the White Pass & Yukon Route railway, Pullen rented a large home in Skagway to start a boarding house. She constructed furniture from packing crates and apple boxes, then later leased furniture that had been intended for a Skagway dance hall. A few years later, Pullen bought the house she'd been renting and turned it into Skagway's finest hotel. She added to the building several times and attracted prominent guests from all over the world, including President Warren Harding.

White Pass & Yukon Route Connects Skagway with Whitehorse
White Pass Depot, 1st Avenue, Skagway

Captain Billy Moore, the first resident of Skagway, began promoting the idea of a railroad leading to the headwaters of the Yukon River nearly a decade before the Klondike Stampede. Once the gold rush began, shipping on the Yukon River boomed. Now, Moore's railroad, which would replace the long ocean and river route to Dawson City through St. Michael, seemed not only feasible but almost imperative.

The White Pass seemed a reasonable choice for a railroad route. The Chilkoot Pass was too steep, rocky and snowy, and the Chilkat, north of Haines Mission, was too far from the Yukon River. Some suggested building a railroad along the Stikine River from Wrangell, while others said the Taku River could be used. All other possibilities looked almost ridiculously unsuitable. By comparison the White Pass, although difficult, seemed the least troublesome.

White Pass & Yukon Route train as it leaves the White Pass summit in June 1890.

The White Pass & Yukon Route was organized in 1898. Even then, the first group of surveyors sent in to do the preliminary field work left with the firm conviction that a railroad couldn't be built over the mountainous terrain. A chance encounter at Skagway with Michael J. Heney, a Canadian contractor who had worked on the construction of the Canadian Pacific Railway, changed their minds.

Hiring Heney to take charge of the railroad's construction, the new company bought four miles (six km) of wagon road that George Brackett had already built from Skagway toward the pass. Although the railroad hadn't as yet obtained a right-of-way through the pass from the Canadian and American governments, Heney commenced construction. By late July 1898, rails had been laid over Brackett's wagon road and the new railroad began carrying passengers that far.

By February 1899 track reached the White Pass summit, and by July it reached Lake Bennett. Another crew had begun construction of track going from Whitehorse toward Skagway. The two work gangs finally met at Carcross on July 29, 1900. Unlike most railroads, the White Pass & Yukon Route made money as it was being built by carrying paying customers over sections of already completed track during the two years of its construction. By the time trains could travel the full distance between Skagway and Whitehorse, the White Pass & Yukon Route, one of the few railroads in North America to have been built without government subsidy, had already recouped its construction costs.

One of the most immediate effects of the railroad's construction was that it ended competition between Skagway and Dyea for Yukon-bound travelers and freight. With a railroad at Skagway, the Chilkoot Trail was no longer a practical route to the interior. In a last-minute attempt to save their community, residents of Dyea, mostly Americans, petitioned the United States government to cede the town to Canada—from the inlet back over the Chilkoot to the Canadian boundary. This would have made Dyea Canada's only seaport on the north Pacific, which perhaps would have been enough to ensure the town's survival. The Americans ignored the request, however, and gradually Dyea became a ghost town. Meanwhile, Skagway's future as a permanent settlement, not merely a boom-and-bust gold rush town, was assured.

Although the White Pass & Yukon Route ceased regular operations between Skagway and Whitehorse in 1978, excursion trains still leave the Skagway depot throughout the summer, taking passengers to the White Pass Summit or on to Lake Bennett, the old starting point for gold stampeders rafting or boating down the Yukon River to Dawson City.

Molly Walsh Murdered
Molly Walsh Park, 6th Avenue, Skagway

Molly Walsh was a dance-hall girl from Butte, Montana, who came north and opened a grub tent on the White Pass Trail. Molly was liked by everyone and had several suitors. Jack Newman and Mike Bartlett were two of the most ardent. Both men amassed comfortable fortunes by running packing businesses over the White Pass during the gold rush, but Molly chose to marry Bartlett. Molly moved to Seattle with her new husband, and not long afterward, for reasons unknown, Bartlett murdered her. Eventually he was convicted, and eventually Newman married someone else, but Newman's memories of Molly never faded. Her tragic fate weighed heavily on his mind all his life, and a couple of years before his death in 1931, Newman erected a monument in Skagway dedicated to her memory.

Bank Makes Money on Robbery
5th Avenue, Skagway

Most frontier towns have a bank robbery or two in their history, but a robbery in Skagway in 1902 left the Canadian Imperial Bank of Commerce richer than it had been before the holdup. Just before closing time on September 15, a man carrying a revolver in one hand and two sticks of dynamite in the other entered the bank and demanded $20,000.

Before any money was obtained, a customer came in the front door. Seeing his opportunity, one of the two employees on duty at the time made a dash for the back door. The robber fired his gun, evidently intending to shoot the escaping employee, but the bullet struck a dynamite stick in his other hand. The resulting explosion killed the robber and blew the customer back out the front door and the escaping employee into the bank's backyard. The other employee was in the safe, where he was found dazed but uninjured.

Although still standing, the building was in shambles. Its windows were broken, money was scattered through the rubble and $2,800 in gold dust from the teller's cage had been blown everywhere. The two bank employees recovered all the cash, but collecting the gold dust proved to be more difficult. First the fire department had to spray the inside of the bank, washing all the dust and debris outside. Then they dug up $4 - 6"$ (10 – 15 cm) of the dirt around the bank and hauled it to the creek. Here, they panned the dirt for the lost gold. In the end, the extra effort was worthwhile because the bank recovered several hundred dollars more in gold dust than it had lost.

Soapy Smith Shoots It Out with Frank Reid
Gold Rush Cemetery, State Street, 1.5 miles (2.4 km) north of Skagway (watch for the sign just before the bridge)

This cemetery is the final resting place for Skagway desperado Soapy Smith and for Frank Reid, the man who killed him in a shoot-out on the Skagway waterfront on July 8, 1898. It was said in Skagway that Frank Reid was the only man who made Soapy Smith even a little bit wary. For months Reid had been at the head of a group of citizens trying, without much success, to get rid of Soapy and his gang. Then on July 7, just three days after Soapy led the Skagway Independence Day Parade, his empire began to fall apart.

It all started when J.D. Stewart, a Canadian prospector, came over the White Pass from Dawson City. Stewart was not one of the wildly successful miners of the Klondike, but he did have a poke of gold worth almost $3,000. When he came into Skagway on his way home to Nanaimo, British Columbia, Stewart happened to meet the "Reverend" Charles Bowers, one of Soapy's con men. Bowers convinced Stewart to take his gold to Old Man Tripp, another of Soapy's benevolent con men, who was posing as a gold buyer. Between them, Tripp and Bowers convinced Stewart that he should go to Jeff Smith's Parlor to exchange his gold for cash. Here, another member of the gang, dressed as a returning miner, grabbed Stewart's poke, ran out the back door and disappeared through a secret gate in an otherwise walled-in backyard.

Stewart took his case to a United States deputy marshall, who, of course, was on Soapy Smith's payroll. Stewart was not about to be cheated out of his money easily, however. When the deputy marshall wouldn't do anything, he took his cause to Skagway merchants, including the packers, who were just then beginning to do business with miners returning from the Klondike. The last thing the packers and merchants of Skagway needed was for news to spread about robberies in their town. It was already said that the wealthy miners of Dawson City left the country through St. Michael in order to avoid Skagway. Stewart, angry over his loss, would obviously sully the town's reputation further unless something was done to prevent it.

Stewart, in fact, was exactly the sort of victim who, in the past, Soapy Smith would have given money to get out of town or simply murdered. Instead of standing alone, however, Stewart linked up with Frank Reid and several other prominent citizens. All were intent on organizing a vigilante committee to get rid of Soapy Smith. Crowds of people began forming in the street as word spread through town about what had happened.

One of the largest crowds gathered on Broadway in the afternoon of July 8. Suddenly, Soapy himself appeared. He wore a mackinaw coat, and as he walked up to the crowd, he thrust both of his hands into his coat pockets, leaving the pointed outlines of what appeared to be revolvers protruding toward the crowd. Moments before, the mob had been hollering for Soapy Smith's head. Now, standing face to face with the man, they backed down and went their separate ways as Smith spit verbal venom after them.

But Soapy Smith, too, found himself in a corner. He had been asked to return Stewart's poke. Even members of his gang asked him to back down. But the public humiliation such an act entailed was too much for him to endure. Soapy Smith had come to Skagway masquerading as an upright citizen, and in his mind he had become that citizen. Soapy decided to stand his ground. He ran into Frank Reid on the street and challenged him to fight. Reid, unarmed at the time, went home and got a gun, but when he went to Soapy's parlor, Soapy wasn't there.

As the evening wore on, it was reported that Soapy, who was generally thought of as an abstainer, was at his parlor drinking whiskey. Already members of his gang were slipping away into the mountains to hide. It was said that one, Tim Vogel, walked all the way from Skagway to Haines Mission, an arduous 50 miles (80 km) or so of tidal flats, jagged shoreline and rugged coastal forest. A public meeting began to form on the wharf, with Frank Reid, Si Tanner and several others standing guard to see that none of Soapy's men tried to disrupt the proceedings.

When Soapy got word of the meeting, he grabbed a Winchester rifle and a Colt .45 revolver from behind the bar and headed for the dock, staggering down Skagway's main street, muttering and swearing drunkenly about what he intended to do to anyone who got in his way. When he reached the waterfront, Soapy went straight for Frank Reid. Eyewitnesses said the two men were only an arm's length apart when Soapy leveled his Winchester at Reid's head. Reid grabbed the muzzle of Soapy's rifle with his right hand and pushed it toward the ground as he reached for his revolver with his left.

Reid evidently pulled the trigger first, but his gun misfired. Soapy swung the rifle back up and shot Reid in the groin. Reid then fired three more times, hitting Soapy point-blank with all three shots. Almost instantly, Skagway's most notorious and, at times, charming bad man was dead. Reid hung on for nearly two weeks before he, too, succumbed to his wounds.

Stampeders Cross Mountains on Chilkoot Pass
Klondike Highway, .5 miles (.8 km) north of junction with Dyea Road; 2.5 miles (4 km) north of Skagway

A plaque here commemorates the men and women who took part in the great Klondike Gold Rush of 1897–98. Various estimates, some as high as 500,000, have been given for the number of people who actually set out for the Yukon during the gold rush. Most never made it out of the lower 48 states or southern Canada. Of the 40,000 or so who actually reached Dawson City, most got there after crossing the Coast Mountains over the Chilkoot or White Pass. And the vast majority of these, probably at least 25,000, came by the Chilkoot Trail from Dyea, two miles (three km) west of this point.

An endless line of stampeders climb the Chilkoot Pass in the spring of 1898.

Once the stampede started, the White Pass turned out to be an unreliable route for the large numbers of people attempting to cross the mountains. Mud slides regularly closed it for days and weeks at a time—and closed it completely through the autumn of 1897. Most of the stampeders gave up on the White Pass and headed for Dyea. Ironically, the undependable White Pass contributed to Skagway's growth instead of Dyea's during the first year of the gold rush. Lying at the head of the White Pass, Skagway was constantly swelled with argonauts unable to move forward because traffic on the trail had ground to a halt. Dyea, on the other hand, saw a comparatively steady stream of stampeders pass through unimpeded because the Chilkoot was usually open.

Today probably no image of the Klondike Gold Rush comes to mind quicker than the famous photograph of the endless gray line of stampeders hunched under their heavy loads as they climbed one behind another toward the snow-covered summit of the Chilkoot Pass. Certainly no other part of the Klondike Stampede symbolizes so completely the immensity of the undertaking that participating in the Klondike Gold Rush entailed or the tremendous obstacles that confronted each of the stampeders. Nothing demonstrates so graphically the grit and persistence required to get to the Klondike or the determination required of the men and women who carried their 2,000 pounds (907 kilograms) of supplies over the Chilkoot.

The Chilkoot Pass through the mountains to the Yukon had been used for centuries by the Tlingit Indians of the Alaska coast as a trade route to the inland Indians. To preserve their monopoly on that trade, the Tlingit banned everyone else, white and Indian alike, from the trail for years. Keeping Yukon Indians on their side of the pass guaranteed the Tlingit an inland market for products obtained on the coast. When Russians began trading in Alaska, the Tlingit quickly added European goods to the trade articles they carried over the pass. But no Russian (or, later, American) traders were ever allowed to cross and compete in that trade.

In the 1880s the Tlingit came across a new breed of white man in the Yukon interior. These men had come not to trade but to prospect for gold. Since they weren't competitors for the trade with the interior Indians, they posed no obvious threat to the Tlingit. Barring them from the trail seemed unnecessary. Then the Tlingit discovered they could make more money carrying goods over the pass for the miners than they could hauling their own trade goods across for the inland Indians. Once that happened restrictions on travel over the Chilkoot gradually disappeared.

Long before the gold rush started in 1897, the Chilkoot had become the primary route to the upper Yukon River for white miners. Once the stampede started, the Tlingit tribes (Chilkoot, Chilkat and Stikines) profited as never before. A constant stream of humanity went over the pass between the summers of 1897 and 1898. As the numbers increased, so did the prices the Tlingit charged for packing goods over the trail.

Of all the participants in the great Klondike Gold Rush, the Tlingit were among the few who actually made money. Years before, a miner had cheated one of them by paying with Confederate cash. As a consequence none of the Tlingit would accept paper currency. The extent of Tlingit fortunes can be seen in the gold and silver coin shortage that soon developed in Dyea and Skagway, where the stampeders found it increasingly difficult to scrape together enough hard money to pay the packers.

The Tlingit were not, of course, the only ones to make money during the gold rush. Other enterprising people found way to turn disadvantages to good fortune. Although, for instance, the first few miles of the Chilkoot Trail were deceptively easy, as it began to climb, the true nature of the pass began to present itself. As the weeks wore on, the sides of the trail became littered with all manner of goods left behind to lighten loads. Two quick-witted storekeepers went up and down the trail collecting discarded overshoes, which they then took back to Juneau to resell to stampeders in need of rubber boots. Other items were also collected and resold.

The typical stampeder took three months to pack his ton of supplies across to Lake Bennett and the head of navigation on the Yukon River. Upon completing the final assault on the summit—a 10-hour climb carrying as much as 75 pounds (34 kilograms) a trip—the argonaut would deposit his goods, then turn and slide back down the pass on his bottom, toboggan-style, for another load. Most attempted only one trip to the summit each day.

At just about any time from the summer of 1897 through the summer of 1898, several thousand people could be found spread along the 35 miles (56 km) of trail between Dyea and Lake Bennett. Small communities of tents grew up from one end of the trail to the other.

As is always the case where large numbers of people gather, enterprising souls of one shade or another soon set themselves up in business, catering to the crowds along the trail. Bunco men and gamblers often worked at little more than wide spots in the path. Saloons, hotels, brothels and makeshift restaurants appeared. The Palmers, a farm couple from Wisconsin with seven children, ran completely out of money while they were at Sheep Camp just four miles (six km) below the summit of the pass. In desperation they opened a "hotel" in an improvised shack. Almost immediately they began taking in a small fortune. Dubbed the Palmer House, the hotel fed an estimated 500 people a day at its peak and housed 40 guests each night.

As the winter progressed, stampeders walked in an ever deepening trench as the sides of the trail grew higher and higher with snow. Two men cut steps in the ice over the last 150 feet (46M) of the climb, then charged a small sum of money to anyone who wanted to use the steps. Their enterprise brought in $80 a day in tolls. Other entrepreneurs followed their lead.

Travel became easier in December 1897, when the first tramway was built. By May, five of them operated between Canyon City—at about the halfway point on the western side of the pass—and the Chilkoot summit.

Despite the large numbers of people on the Chilkoot Trail, there were relatively few deaths. The greatest tragedy occurred on April 3, 1898. Winter storms had packed the pass with snow. Several more feet of heavy wet snow had fallen during the previous two weeks. The Indians and experienced packers refused to continue packing. In spite of their warnings stampeders, anxious to get going again during a break in the snowfall, headed for the summit.

Early on a Sunday morning, April 3, the faint rumbles of avalanches in the high passes could be heard. People on the trails stopped to listen at first, then began to flee. Before everyone could escape, however, a huge avalanche crashed down, covering 10 acres (4 ha) of the trail with 30 feet (9M) of wet snow. Only a few of the people buried were rescued. More than 60 died, most suffocating under the heavy snow. Many were dug up with their bodies still in a running position. Within a few days, however, stampeders were once more crossing the Chilkoot Pass on their way to Dawson City.

Captain Moore Discovers Dead Horse Trail

Captain William Moore Bridge, Klondike Highway, 10.5 miles (17 km) north of Skagway

This bridge on Moore Creek is named for the founder of Skagway, Captain Billy Moore. Moore first settled in what would become Skagway in the autumn of 1887. Earlier that summer, Skookum Jim, a Tagish Indian, had led him through the White Pass, which, in the curious ways of Western history, allowed Moore to claim credit for the discovery of the pass.

Moore's new mountain pass was used very little during the following decade, but when the gold rush of 1897 came along everything changed. Suddenly, Moore's trail was touted as the easiest way over the mountains into the interior. Unfortunately, with increased traffic on the pass, the often narrow winding trail soon turned into a torturous series of mud holes and steep rocky pathways. For the first few miles out of Skagway, the trail followed the river and was relatively easy. But then it began a winding up-and-down course over a series of boulder-strewn hills with long descents into river bogs and marshland. Often the trail narrowed between river and rock until there was barely room for a horse to pass.

On Devil's Hill there were places in the trail barely two feet (.6M) wide, places where a horse's single misstep could toss the animal to its death 500 feet (152M) below. On the western side of the pass the continual rains shut out the sun and turned the trampled ground to rivers of mud. The last few miles before the summit were by far the worst. Swollen by coastal rains, frigid creeks as much as 20 feet (6M) wide gushed down the mountainside, cutting through the trail in torrents chest deep. There were no bridges, so stampeders waded the icy waters of each creek before climbing the rocky incline to the summit. It was a trail to exhaust even the strongest of men.

Since much of the trail was too narrow for one animal to pass another, traffic was painfully slow at the best of times and often stopped completely. Day in and day out the long line of marchers started, stopped, restarted and stopped again—worse than any rush-hour traffic jam city commuters face today.

Horses stood for hours without being unloaded because their owners were afraid the long lineup would start without them. The animals suffered tragically along the trail. Many of them were old and worn out when they were bought in Victoria, Seattle or other West Coast cities. On the trail, their new owners generally knew nothing about animal care. With few exceptions the horses were underfed, and sometimes they stood for hours in the freezing rain, straining under the weight of their often poorly packed loads. When they were finally allowed to move again, they were driven over narrow trails hock deep in mud or up rocky escarpments that scraped and cut their legs and feet. Horses that collapsed on the trail were shot where they fell while their owners tore the loads from their backs and stashed the supplies before returning to the coast for another horse. Meanwhile, the procession would continue relentlessly over the top of the dead animal lying in its path.

Hundreds of horses died in this manner on the White Pass in the autumn of 1897. According to many witnesses, some of the animals flung themselves over the sides of the ravines, apparently committing suicide rather than facing more time on what people were already calling the Dead Horse Trail. Horses that made it over the White Pass to Lake Bennett fared no better. Here, men anxious to get on to the gold fields abandoned them to starve.

Jack London wrote that horses

from Skagway to Bennett rotted in heaps. They died at the rocks, they were poisoned at the summit, and they starved at the lakes; they fell off the trail ... [and] in the river they drowned under their loads or were smashed to pieces against the boulders; they snapped their legs in the crevices and broke their backs falling backward with their packs; in the sloughs they sank from fright or smothered in the slime; and they were disemboweled in the bogs where the corduroy logs turned end up in the mud. ...

By September 1897 the White Pass mercifully closed until winter temperatures froze the ground enough to allow renewed access. Then thousands more took to the trail again. As they marched back and forth, getting their ton of supplies to Lake Bennett, the trail through the mountains slowly rose literally above the land. Normally, much of the nearly continuous snowfall on the mountain pass was blown into the valleys below. But on the White Pass in the winter of 1897–98, where people packed the snow under their feet before it could blow away, the trail rose little by little over the course of the winter until, by spring, it stood 10 feet (3M) higher than the landscape around it.

The gold seekers were so closely packed together on the trail that, at times, if one of them stepped out of line or slipped off the trail to the ground below, he or she might have to wait several hours before a space big enough to rejoin the stampeders opened again. For every two who started on the White Pass, one made it and one turned back in despair.

By the summer of 1898 work began on the White Pass & Yukon Route railway. The new railroad ended traffic on the Chilkoot Trail almost immediately, and it soon replaced the horror of the Dead Horse Trail with a train ride through the spectacular countryside of the White Pass.

North-West Mounted Police Take Possession of Pass Summits

White Pass Summit, Klondike Highway, 14 miles (23 km) north of Skagway

---

Before the Klondike Gold Rush began, the exact location of the Alaska–Canada boundary was unsettled, but the issue seemed relatively unimportant to diplomats from both countries, and no serious attempts had been made to resolve the matter. The Klondike Stampede changed everything. The Americans claimed the border was logically on the eastern side of the mountains at the head of navigation on the Yukon River at Lake Bennett. The Canadians just as obstinately said the boundary as set out in an earlier treaty with Russia lay west of present-day Skagway in a straight line between the 141st Meridian on the Alaska coast and the top of Portland Canal.

With no progress on the issue in sight, the Canadian government ordered the North-West Mounted Police to take possession of the mountain passes in February 1898. Reasoning that possession was nine-tenths of the law and that the passes seemed a reasonable compromise, the Mounties took their position at the head of the White and Chilkoot passes. Here, the police greeted American stampeders as they arrived in Canada, collected any duties owing on the goods brought into the country and bid the argonauts on their way. It was a compromise location, but in the end it suited both governments.

White Pass & Yukon Route Connects Skagway and Whitehorse
Klondike Highway, 22.5 miles (36 km) north of Skagway

The White Pass & Yukon Route railway reached the summit of White Pass in February 1899. The entire distance between Skagway and Whitehorse was completed by the summer of 1900, just two years after construction began.

This particular section of track between Log Cabin and the White Pass summit was especially difficult to build. According to the company's first president, Samuel Haughton Graves, on this stretch of track there wasn't a "wheelbarrow full of gravel or loose earth . . . the line is entirely on solid rock or bridges." To add to the troubles the builders had cutting their way through this rock, blasting and construction of the line took place over the winter of 1898–99, a particularly cold and snowy year.

In 1994 the White Pass & Yukon Route was designated an International Historic Civil Engineering Landmark by the Canadian and American societies of civil engineering.

Montana Mountain Yields Gold and Silver
Klondike Highway, 51.5 miles (83 km) north of Skagway

The first gold claim on Montana Mountain was made by W.R. Young in 1899. By 1905 most of the claims in the area had been bought up by Conrad Consolidated Mines, which began exploration and mining operations that year. Montana Mountain and Montana Creek were named for the home state of Conrad Mines developer John Howard Conrad. Conrad City, a town of about 300 people, was built along Windy Arm, an extension of Tagish Lake. The Venus Mill, the ruins of which can be seen near the sign, was built in 1908. An aerial tramway transported silver ore from the mountain to the mill, where it was bagged, then shipped to Carcross by boat and from there to tidewater at Skagway on the railroad.

In 1911 bankruptcy closed Conrad Consolidated. Other small mining concerns continued over the years, including the Venus Mines, which operated between 1979 and 1981. Then falling silver prices made mining operations unprofitable.

Frederick Schwatka Maps Yukon River
Klondike Highway, 59 miles (95 km) north of Skagway

In 1883, Lieutenant Frederick Schwatka of the United States Army became the first man to explore and map the entire length of the Yukon River. Schwatka, who had previously traveled in the North with a search party hunting for the lost Franklin Expedition, was not on an official expedition of the United States government. His commanding officer, General Nelson Miles of Indian-fighting fame had sponsored the trip himself. Miles felt Alaska fell within his command although no American troops were stationed there at the time. The general was interested in the far northwest and had tried for years without success to get the army to mount an expedition to the Yukon River. Finally, in exasperation, Miles arranged for Schwatka to go north without proper authorization, paying for the trip from his own pocket. When it became known that Schwatka had crossed the Chilkoot to explore the Yukon on the Canadian side of the boundary, both the U.S. Congress and Miles were embarrassed by the incident, although Miles defended his subordinate.

After Schwatka and his men crossed the Chilkoot Pass, they followed the lakes to the Yukon River as thousands of stampeders would do 15 years later. Schwatka named Lake Lindemann for the secretary of the Bremen Geographical Society in Germany. Lake Bennett he named for a newspaper reporter. When he passed near the mouth of Windy Arm on Tagish Lake in 1883, Schwatka named Bove Island after an Italian Navy Lieutenant.

Actually, he named the whole of Tagish Lake after the Lieutenant. Schwatka became notorious for naming every geographical feature in sight, while ignoring any names the miners or aboriginal people already used. The name Tagish Lake, which had been in common use before Schwatka mapped the area, was reinstated by George Dawson when he and William Ogilvie surveyed and mapped the Yukon for the Canadian government in 1887. Bove Island, however, remained as Schwatka's memorial to the Italian lieutenant. There is no record of what the Tagish people originally called the lake or the island.

Caribou Crossing at Carcross
Klondike Highway, Carcross

The town of Carcross was originally known as Caribou Crossing because caribou used to cross here at the Nares River between Bennett and Tagish lakes in the 19th century. Native people had sporadically camped in the area for centuries, but the town didn't really start until the Klondike Gold Rush. Then the narrows here provided a convenient layover spot for stampeders on their way to Dawson City. The North-West Mounted Police also built a post here in 1898.

The small settlement became a town once the White Pass & Yukon Route railway was built. Many of its initial residents were drawn from a Tagish Indian village once located a few miles east of here. The new Indian residents, like most of the whites, moved to Caribou Crossing to be closer to the railroad.

The name *Caribou Crossing* was shortened to Carcross in 1904 when Bishop Bompas of the Church of England complained that his mail was often mistakenly sent to the British Columbia Cariboo region instead of the Yukon. Postal authorities accepted the Bishop's suggestion that the name be shortened.

Although the town's original name derives from the caribou crossing, no caribou have been seen here since the turn of the century.

Polly the Parrot Dies in Carcross
Klondike Highway, Carcross

One of Carcross's most famous residents was a foul-mouthed parrot named Polly. Captain James Alexander had carried the bird over the Chilkoot Pass in 1898. In 1918 Alexander left her at the Caribou Hotel in Carcross for what was to have been a temporary stay while he left the Yukon for a short time, traveling south from Skagway on the ship *Princess Sophia.*

Unfortunately, the *Princess Sophia* sank, and all on board were lost. Polly lived out her life in Carcross at the Caribou Hotel. In her early years she was known for her hard drinking, which she gave up later in life, and for her ability to speak Italian, sing operatic arias and swear like a sailor.

Eventually, Polly stopped talking to adults except when tourists would ask if she wanted a cracker. Then she'd scream, "Go to hell." Otherwise Polly talked only with children. She died at the age of 125 in 1972. Her grave and a small bronze plaque can be found at the local cemetery.

Carcross Home to Klondike Gold Discoverers
Klondike Highway, Carcross

Skookum Jim, the original discoverer of gold on Bonanza Creek, was from a Tagish Indian village a few miles east of the present town of Carcross. When the White Pass & Yukon Route railway was completed, residents of the village moved to the new village of Carcross, and Skookum Jim came with them.

Skookum Jim, with his Klondike wealth, built the biggest house in town. He furnished the house quite ornately by Yukon standards. The chairs at the dining-room table had mother-of-pearl inlays, and his silverware was encrusted with gold nuggets he had brought back from his Klondike mine. On a trip to Vancouver in 1902, Jim bought a Persian rug for $2,000, but when he got the rug home it turned out to be a bit big for the living room. Jim was about to cut the carpet to make it fit, but his wife stopped him. She didn't want the rug damaged, so Jim had the house enlarged to fit the carpet.

Dawson Charlie, who discovered gold along with George Carmack and Skookum Jim in the Klondike, also lived in Carcross, although the house he built was not as large as Skookum Jim's. Dawson Charlie, who before the gold strike had been known as Tagish Charlie, also built the Caribou Hotel in Carcross. He and Skookum Jim often went on gold prospecting trips even after they had found wealth on Bonanza Creek. Together, they discovered gold in the Kluane area of the Yukon in 1903. This discovery touched off another smaller gold rush, although in the end the area proved to be of little mineral value.

Dawson Charlie fell off the bridge in Carcross in the early morning after Christmas in 1909, probably after a night of drinking. Skookum Jim lived until 1916, when he also died in Carcross. Unlike the vast majority of those who made fortunes in the Klondike, Jim had not spent all his money during his life. He left most of the remainder of his estate in a trust fund "to be devoted toward medical attendance [and] supplying necessities and comforts to Indians in the Yukon Territory."

Last Spike at Carcross
White Pass & Yukon Route Railway Depot, Carcross

A cairn beside the railroad station in Carcross commemorates the driving of the last spike on the White Pass & Yukon Route. Crews working from Whitehorse and Skagway met here on July 29, 1900. The railroad had taken just over two years to build, and a golden spike was made for the occasion.

The official ceremony turned out to be a spirited affair involving dignitaries from both Canada and the United States. When it came time to drive the golden spike into the final tie, none of the VIPs seemed up to the task. Their many blows bent, sideswiped and bounced off the yellow nail, but all they succeeded in doing was flattening the gilded spire against the tie. Afterward, they left in high spirits for further celebrations. As they departed, a railroad worker pried up the mangled gold, gave it to a company official, then drove home a traditional iron spike.

World's Smallest Desert in Yukon
Klondike Highway, 1 mile (1.6 km) north of Carcross

A large glacial lake that once covered this area left behind sand dunes east of the highway here. Winds off Lake Bennett keep most vegetation, other than lodgepole pine and kinnikinnick, from becoming established. This gives the area, with its rolling dunes and sparse vegetation, a desertlike appearance. Equal to about one section of land (640 acres / 240 ha), it is commonly called the world's smallest desert.

Yukon River First Known as Lewes
Lewes (Lewis) Creek, Highway 2, 13.5 miles (22 km) north of Carcross

In 1843 Robert Campbell of the Hudson's Bay Company

became the first explorer to reach the Yukon River after he had followed the Pelly River to its mouth on the Yukon. But instead of realizing he had reached a new and larger river, Campbell decided that the Yukon, which he called the Lewes, was simply a tributary of the Pelly. Everything on today's Yukon above the junction with the Pelly, Campbell called the Lewes; everything downstream he called the Pelly.

Even when it was discovered that the junction of the Porcupine and "Youcon" at Fort Yukon was the same river as Campbell's Pelly (as was the Russians' Quikpok), the name Lewes persisted for the upper portion of the stream as far as Lake Laberge. The river above Laberge was known as the Thirtymile.

In 1883 Lieutenant Schwatka of the United States Army became the first person to travel the length of today's Yukon River, mapping its entire course as the Yukon. Not until 1945, however, did the Canadian government officially change the name from Lewes to Yukon.

Today, only this small creek and a nearby lake still bear the name Lewes and even Lewes Creek and Lewes Lake have a tenuous hold on their names. Instead of being christened with the early name of the great Yukon River, they were actually named for A.B. Lewis, a construction engineer working on the White Pass & Yukon Route railroad. Lewis inadvertently drained 50 feet (15M) of the lake during the building of the railroad, so the lake was named after him. Early in the century, though, another mistake—this time on official maps—incorrectly called the lake and creek "Lewes." The name has been mistakenly printed that way on maps ever since.

Stikine Bill Robinson Bribes Mounties
Highway 2, 21 miles (34 km) north of Carcross

The railroad siding of Robinson was named for White Pass & Yukon Route railway employee Stikine Bill Robinson. Gold was discovered nearby and a townsite was constructed in the early 1900s, but low yields led to its abandonment by 1915. When the townspeople moved away, the newly unemployed postmaster started one of the first cattle ranches in the Yukon.

A tale told about Stikine Bill Robinson and the building of the White Pass & Yukon Route asserts that the Mounted Police initially blocked construction of the railroad at the international boundary because Ottawa had never sent official word that the railroad was to proceed. Railway officials tried everything they could think of to get the Mounties to change their minds, but the police wouldn't budge.

Then Mike Heney, the company official overseeing construction, got his enterprising friend Stikine Bill Robinson to pay the Mounties a visit. Robinson made the trip to the summit with a bottle of Scotch in each pocket of his mackinaw and a box of cigars under each arm. No mention was ever made again of construction delays while waiting for word from Ottawa.

Alaska Highway Built in Eight Months

Junction of the Klondike and Alaska Highways, 32.5 miles (52 km) north of Carcross

The Klondike and Alaska highways connect at this point. For the next 20.5 miles (33 km) the two roads follow the same route north until they separate again on the northwest side of Whitehorse. At that point the Alaska Highway curves west toward Haines Junction and the Alaska border while the Klondike Highway turns north again toward Dawson City.

The United States Army cut the original Alaska Highway through the wilds of British Columbia, the Yukon and Alaska in just eight months, beginning in March 1942. A land connection between the United States, southern Canada and Alaska seemed imperative after the Japanese attack on Pearl Harbor on December 7, 1941. The construction of the first tote road between Dawson Creek, British Columbia, and Delta, Alaska, is considered an engineering marvel because of the lengthy wilderness terrain it crosses and the speed with which the work was completed.

But the Alaska Highway was not an entirely new road. For much of the way, construction of the highway involved connecting and upgrading a series of existing trails and wagon roads. After the tote road had been completed, civilian contractors improved and upgraded the highway during the war. In 1946, the American army turned the Canadian portion of the highway over to the Canadian government.

McCrae a Supply Point for Alaska Highway Construction
Klondike–Alaska Highways, 5.5 miles (9 km) north of junction of Alaska–Klondike Highway south

McCrae was a railroad town founded in 1900 when it became a whistle-stop on the new White Pass & Yukon Route railway. When construction of the Alaska Highway began, McCrae turned out to be strategically located where the railroad would first cross the proposed highway. This instantly transformed the old railway stopping point into a major service and supply point for American military construction crews. A large camp was built, and McCrae became the destination for tens of thousands of pounds of freight shipped in on the railroad from Skagway.

In addition to its role as a supply point for the construction of the Alaska Highway, McCrae supplied construction crews working on the Canol Road and Pipeline. (More information about McCrae and the Canol Road can be found in Part II, the Alaska Highway.)

Jack London Pilots Boats through Miles Canyon
Klondike–Alaska Highways, 7 miles (11 km) north of the southern junction of the two highways
Camera viewpoint sign marks turnoff road to Miles Canyon. Follow turnoff to fork in road, then follow right-hand fork .5 miles (.8 km) to parking lot near canyon

In 1897–98 Miles Canyon and the White Horse Rapids just below it provided the first rough water on the Yukon after stampeders who had crossed the Chilkoot or White Pass took to the river. Most of the stampeders stopped at Lindemann or Bennett Lake to build their boats. From the lakes they descended into the river system, floating downstream to Dawson City. Most were inexperienced boatbuilders and oarsmen. In fact, the armada that started down the Yukon in the spring of 1898 might well have been the largest, most unseaworthy fleet of boats ever created. Constructed from green lumber that the stampeders had whip-sawed from the small spruce near the lake shore, the sailing craft were of every imaginable size and description. Because of the green lumber, all the boats leaked, and because of poor construction, many of them sank.

Whipsawing proved to be a severe strain on partnerships. The task called for one man to stand on top of the sawpit frame, on the high side of the log, pulling the saw up while guiding it down. The other man stood below, pulling the saw down on the cutting stroke, pushing it up on the return. The man below contended with sawdust falling constantly into his face, and neither man could ever be sure his partner was pulling and pushing his fair share of the load. All through the winter of 1897–98, as the men worked on the boats in preparation for the spring breakup on the river, partnership after partnership dissolved in rancor.

One pair grew so angry at each other that they literally divided their goods in half. So strict were the terms of the separation that each man got exactly half the flour, half the bacon, half the tent and half the new boat they'd just finished building. The boat was sawed lengthwise, leaving each partner with one side.

The ice went out of the lakes on May 29, and 800 boats took to the water for Dawson City. Within two days, more than 7,000 boats and 30,000 stampeders were on their way to the Klondike. At Miles Canyon, 150 boats were wrecked and five men lost their lives. Then the North-West Mounted Police stepped in to ensure that only seaworthy boats with competent pilots went through the canyon and over the rapids. Many of the stampeders simply portaged to the north side of the rapids.

The previous autumn, Jack London, a 21-year-old ex-sailor, had been one of the first stampeders to take a boat through the canyon without mishap. An experienced boatman, London had no trouble piloting his well-made craft through the canyon and down the White Horse Rapids just below it on the river.

After London became famous as a writer of stories about the Yukon, a gold rush legend developed that had him stopping on his way north to spend several days piloting the boats of other less-experienced stampeders through the rapids. According to the story, London made $3,000 for this work. But the tale is a fabrication. Although London never refuted the story, he actually only piloted his own boat through the rapids. Then briefly interrupting his race to get downriver before freeze-up, he went back and took the boat of a friend through the rapids. No money changed hands. In fact London, after spending a winter in the Yukon, went home nearly broke, not making a cent from his Klondike adventure. In San Francisco he had to sell the $4.50 worth of gold dust he brought back just to get money for food.

Within a few years, however, London was to claim that although he never made any money mining gold in the Yukon, his books about the North allowed him, for years afterward, "to pan out a living . . . on the strength of that trip."

Railroad, Highway and Steamboats Bring Prominence to Whitehorse
Klondike–Alaska Highway, Whitehorse

The point of land just below Miles Canyon and the White Horse Rapids was the practical head of navigation on the Yukon River during the gold rush of 1897–98. A tent town called White Horse City grew up on the east side of the river in today's Riverdale section of Whitehorse, and a tramway was built around Miles Canyon and the White Horse Rapids. Once the White Pass & Yukon Route railway decided to build the terminus of the new railroad on the north side of the rapids, however, a permanent town developed.

When railroad officials surveyed a townsite on the west side of the river in 1899, they named the new settlement Closeleigh after the Close brothers of England, two of the company's most prominent investors. But William Ogilvie, the commissioner of the Yukon, didn't like the name. He had postal officials name the place White Horse, after the rapids and the original tent town. Later, the name was shortened to one word.

As the distribution center for the entire region, Whitehorse grew rapidly. In the winter, passengers and freight destined for Dawson City and other Yukon communities were sent overland on the Dawson Trail. Once the ice was off the river, however, the busy Yukon shipping season began. The British Yukon Navigation Company, a subsidiary of the White Pass & Yukon Route, operated a fleet of sternwheelers on the Yukon and other rivers in the area.

Although Whitehorse was a railroad town, the major part of its economy was initially based on steamboats and freighting on the Yukon River. In the Yukon, in fact, the era of the steam-driven sternwheeler lasted into the 1950s, when river traffic was finally superseded by the Alaska Highway and other new roads in the territory—especially the Dawson–Mayo Road to White-horse.

First SS *Klondike* Crashes; Second SS *Klondike* Retires
SS Klondike *National Historic Site, next to the Robert Campbell Bridge at Yukon River, Whitehorse*

Steamboats plied the waters of the Yukon River for nearly a century before highways and dependable air service pushed them aside in the early 1950s. Two ships bore the name SS *Klondike*. The first was built in 1929 in Whitehorse. At the time it was the largest boat on the river, but an explosion in 1936 destroyed it.

A second boat, the same size as the first, was built the following year. This boat, now on display in Whitehorse, worked on the Yukon and Stewart rivers until 1952, when most of the ore and supplies going between Dawson, Mayo and Whitehorse were switched to trucks traveling the new Dawson–Mayo Road. For a time the Klondike attempted to run as a tourist boat, but the scheme never paid off. The SS *Klondike* made its last trip in the summer of 1955.

Yukon River Traditional Road to Dawson City
Junction of Alaska Highway and Klondike Highway North

For just about 100 years, from the time Robert Campbell established the first Hudson's Bay Company post on the Yukon

Six stampeders en route to Dawson in 1899.

River at Fort Selkirk until World War II, the Yukon River served as the major highway in Canada's far northwest. For over 50 years, beginning when gold was discovered in the Klondike, the river served as the main link between Whitehorse and Dawson City, 460 miles (740 km) away. But in 1950, a new road was built from Mayo to haul ore from United Keno Mine to Whitehorse. By 1955, the road had been upgraded for automobile traffic and extended to Dawson City, which lead to the disappearance of steamboats from the Yukon.

Takhini Hot Springs Grows Tomatoes for U.S. Army
Takhini Hot Springs Road, Klondike Highway, 4 miles (6 km) north of Alaska Highway Intersection

Takhini Hot Springs have been used by native people for generations. By the 1800s they were known and used by trappers and prospectors. After the gold rush, the hot springs were used by travelers on the Takhini River and on the Dawson Trail between Whitehorse and Dawson City.

During World War II, the United States Army built greenhouses at the springs, using the 117°F (47°C) water as a source of heat. Today, a resort and public pool are located at the springs.

Sam McGee Cremated at Lake Laberge
Historical Marker, Klondike Highway, 20.5 miles (33 km) north of Alaska Highway Intersection, Lake Laberge turnoff, 1.5 miles (2.4 km) down the road to Lake Laberge

Robert Service ensured fame for both himself and Lake Laberge when he wrote "The Cremation of Sam McGee," the first lines of which set the now-famous eerie scene for the rest of the poem:

There are strange things done in the midnight sun
By the men who moil for gold;
The Arctic trails have their secret tales
That would make your blood run cold;
The Northern Lights have seen queer sights,
By the queerest they ever did see

Was the night on the marge of Lake Lebarge
I cremated Sam McGee.

Before Europeans came to the Yukon, the Tagish Indians called the lake *Kluk-tas-si.* The Tlingit called it *Tahini-wud.* Then in 1870 William H. Dall, Director of the Scientific Corps of the Western Union Telegraph Expedition, named it Lake Laberge after Michael Laberge of Chateaugay, Quebec. Laberge had explored part of the Yukon River with Frank Ketchum in 1867, looking for an overland telegraph route to Siberia. Although Laberge may never have seen the lake, he was given a description of it by local Indians and so was able to report its existence to Dall.

Robert Service, the bard of the Yukon, stands on the porch of his famous cabin in Dawson City.

The 30 miles (48 km) of Yukon River flowing between the north end of Lake Laberge and Hootalinqua, at the confluence of the Teslin River, has been designated a Canadian Heritage River. A canoe trip along the route passes abandoned cabins and rotted boats that date from the days of the gold rush.

Frederick Schwatka First to Completely Map Yukon River
Klondike Highway at Fox Lake, 29.5 miles (48 km) north of Alaska Highway Intersection

In 1883, United States Army Lieutenant Frederick Schwatka gave a new name to the body of water local trappers and prospectors had been calling Fox Lake. Schwatka called it *Richthofen,* after a prominent German geographer. Despite his tendency to rename prominent landmarks with monikers of his own choosing—no matter what native people, traders and prospectors might already be calling them—Schwatka can be credited with being the first to travel and map the Yukon River from its headwaters to its outlet at Norton Sound on the Bering Sea.

Even though Schwatka wrote the name *Richthofen* on his map of the Yukon, local people continued to call the place by its earlier name. Finally, in 1957 the name *Fox Lake* was reinstated on official Yukon maps.

Montague House Built on Dawson Trail
Klondike Highway, 81.5 miles (131 km) north of Whitehorse

The Dawson Trail was normally used from October until May, after which summer traffic used the river as the main link between Dawson and Whitehorse. Stopping houses were built along the winter trail at intervals of no more than 20 miles (32 km) over the entire course of the 330-mile (531-km) road. The Montague House, built in 1899, was one of these roadhouses. It provided food and shelter for travelers as well as stables for horses. The shell of the old log structure still stands today.

George Carmack Discovers Gold
Klondike Highway, Carmacks

The town of Carmacks grew up near a trading post originally established by George Washington Carmack in 1893. Carmack had discovered coal on nearby Tantalus Butte and built what was described as the best cabin on the upper Yukon River. He planned to trade furs with local Indians and develop a mine.

Although Carmack never became a successful trader or coal miner, four years after building his trading post, he, along with two of his wife's Tagish relatives, staked the discovery claim on Bonanza Creek in the Klondike. When news of this discovery reached the outside world, the Klondike Gold Rush began.

George Carmack, one of the Klondike's first gold discoverers, standing in front of a log cabin.

Carmack, a Californian whose father had been in the California Gold Rush of 1849, first came to Alaska in 1881 after joining the Marine Corps, which stationed him at Sitka. The next year, after returning to California, he deserted the Corps, then spent two years working on California ranches, saving money to make a return trip to Alaska. Since his youth Carmack had planned to prospect for gold, and in 1885 he once again ventured north. He crossed the Chilkoot Pass and spent the summer prospecting on the upper Yukon River.

Back in Juneau that autumn, after the adventurous but unprofitable months of prospecting, Carmack was nearly broke again. He spent the winter camped near Juneau, eating shellfish and an occasional deer, but the following spring, unable to find work or arrange a grubstake on credit, he moved on to Dyea at the head of Lynn Canal. The Healy and Wilson Trading Post run by John J. Healy, an ex-Montana–Alberta trader, stood at the foot of the pass and was the only white settlement of any kind in the area. It was here that Carmack met Skookum Jim and Tagish Charlie, two Tagish Indians from the southern Yukon who would become his prospecting partners. Ten years later the three men would discover gold in the Klondike.

Carmack, who had learned rudimentary Chinook while in the Marine Corps at Sitka, struck up a friendship with the two Indians at Healy's trading post. The Indians arranged for Carmack to work with them as a packer on the Chilkoot that summer. The following autumn, they invited Carmack to spend the winter with them at their home on Tagish Lake. Carmack accepted the invitation and spent the time learning to trap furs and live in Indian ways.

In the spring of 1887 the three men, along with Jim's sister, Kate, returned to Dyea, where they once more spent the summer working. All four of them hired on with a crew of packers hauling goods for a Canadian government survey party led by William Ogilvie. While Carmack and the rest took the main part of the expedition over the Chilkoot, Skookum Jim led Captain William Moore over the White Pass. Moore was also working with the survey group that summer. He is credited with being the first white man to cross the pass above present-day Skagway.

When Moore met up with the government party at Lake Bennett, he reported to Ogilvie that the new pass was far superior to the Chilkoot. It was lower, Moore said, and even suitable for horses. Moore was so enthusiastic about the new route that at the end of the summer, he returned to the foot of the pass and settled at the mouth of the Skagway River. He was already convinced that large deposits of gold would be discovered in the Yukon. By settling at Skagway, Moore figured that when the gold rush came he would be in control of the most strategic location on the route to the gold fields.

The same autumn that Captain Moore settled in at Skagway, George Carmack moved into a cabin with Jim's sister, Kate, at Dyea. The following spring, in May 1888, Carmack and Kate—accompanied once again by Skookum Jim and Tagish Charlie—crossed the Chilkoot and returned to their Tagish village in the Yukon. A few days later, Jim, Charlie and Carmack left on a summer prospecting trip. This time Carmack explored creeks and rivers as far downstream as the Big Salmon River. Although the three men found trace amounts of gold almost everywhere, the big strike, or even a small profitable one, continued to elude them. The following winter they were back at the Tagish village trapping furs again.

Robert Henderson (center of photo), one of the original discovers of gold in the Klondike region, is seen here with friends in Mayo about 1924.

In the spring of 1889, Carmack sold his share of the furs to Skookum Jim and left with Kate on what turned out to be an extended prospecting trip. The couple went first to the Fortymile District on the Alaska–Yukon border. Here, Carmack spent the summer digging a mine shaft, but when no gold was found, the couple moved on, spending the winter trapping furs along the Porcupine River. The following year they were back at Fortymile, where a new claim yielded enough gold to make wages in a small mining operation.

By the summer of 1892, the claim at Fortymile had been worked out, so the couple moved on. This time they went up the Yukon River as far as the mouth of the Big Salmon. For the next four years Carmack hunted and fished, trapped furs, ran a trading post and even took on odd jobs at Fort Selkirk. All the while, though, he prospected up and down the Yukon River and its tributaries between Fortymile and Big Salmon.

Then, in the summer of 1896, Carmack's Indian relatives and former partners, Tagish Charlie and Skookum Jim, came to visit the Tagish village. No one there had heard from Kate and Carmack in seven years, so Jim and Charlie decided to go looking for them. They found the couple fishing at the mouth of the Klondike River. It was there in August that Carmack resumed his old prospecting partnership with Jim and Charlie.

There are several stories of the Klondike gold discovery. The most likely is that Carmack, Jim and Charlie became interested in the Klondike after another prospector, Robert Henderson, told them about the gold he had discovered along a tributary he called Gold Bottom. Henderson passed by Carmack's fish camp on his way to Gold Bottom, and when Carmack asked if it would be worth his while to stake a claim up there, Henderson reportedly said it would be, but there was no room on the creek for Indians.

A short time later, Jim, Charlie and Carmack started prospecting along Rabbit Creek, a tributary of the Klondike, whose mouth was only about a mile and a half (2.4 km) from the fish camp. The men worked their way up the creek—which would be known as Bonanza within a few more weeks—and then cut along a ridge toward Solomon's Dome. From there they hiked down the Gold Bottom to pay another visit to Henderson, who angered the three miners once again, this time because he refused to sell Skookum Jim some tobacco.

Since the panning on Gold Bottom didn't appear to have been as good as the prospects along Rabbit Creek, Carmack, Jim and Charlie soon started on the return trip to the mouth of the Klondike. Along the way they occasionally stopped to pan for gold, and at Rabbit Creek they decided to camp for the night. Skookum Jim made the actual discovery. He went down to the creek for water, and when he bent down to fill his pan, he saw a wafer of gold between two layers of rock, like cheese in a sandwich, just out of reach in the shallow water beyond the shore.

Although Jim made the discovery, Carmack registered the first claim as well as a second claim allowed by right of discovery. According to Skookum Jim, Carmack registered the discovery claim because he believed that no Indian would be allowed to do it. In later years Carmack claimed that he had, indeed, made the initial gold discovery. No matter who actually saw the gold first, however, proceeds from the claim were divided equally among the men as co-owners of the mine. Tagish Charlie made his own claim at two below discovery and Jim made another claim at one above discovery. (Traditionally, all claims were numbered in relation to their proximity to the first claim staked in an area or along particular creeks.) Carmacks, Jim and Charlie all made small fortunes from their discovery.

Two women wait for customers at the windows of their cabin in Dawson City's Paradise Alley.

In 1898 Carmack left Kate and married Marguerite Laimee, a Dawson City cigar store owner, whose business, like other "cigar stores" in Dawson was actually a front for a house of prostitution. Marguerite, who had gone from gold rush to gold rush, from South Africa to Australia, left with Carmack for Seattle. Here, she managed the Carmack fortune while her husband concentrated on other mining ventures, none of which ever paid off.

Carmack died in 1922 after giving a speech to the local chapter of the Yukon Order of Pioneers in Vancouver, British Columbia. Some time later a statue in his likeness was placed in Pioneer Square in Seattle. The settlement in the Yukon that developed around Carmack's old trading post became an important riverboat stop during and after the gold rush. Later, it became a supply center for mining operations in the area and eventually a major stop on the Klondike Highway between Whitehorse and Dawson City.

Margie Sutherland stands in the doorway of her cigar store in Dawson City in 1899. Most of Dawson's "cigar stores" fronted for houses of prostitution. It is unknown if Margie's was one of these.

Tantalus Butte Out of Reach for Frederick Schwatka
Intersection of Robert Campbell Highway, Klondike Highway, 1 mile (1.6 km) north of Carmacks

Tantalus Butte was another site named by American soldier Frederick Schwatka during his explorations of the Yukon River in 1883. Schwatka chose to call the butte Tantalus because of the way the mountain seemed to appear just ahead on the river and then suddenly disappear behind one of the river's constant twists and turns.

In Greek mythology Tantalus, the son of Zeus and Pluto, steals ambrosia and nectar for mortals. As punishment Zeus consigned him to everlasting torture in the underworld. There, he stands up to his chin in water, but every time he bends to take a drink, the water recedes so he can't taste any. Clusters of fruit hang above his head, but whenever he tries to eat any, the fruit turns out to be too high to reach. In similar fashion, for miles on end, Tantalus Butte seemed just out of reach to Frederick Schwatka.

Robert Campbell Highway Follows Original Route to the Yukon
Intersection of Robert Campbell Highway, Klondike Highway, 1 mile (1.6 km) north of Carmacks

The Robert Campbell Highway runs between the Klondike Highway and Watson Lake. For much of the way, it roughly parallels the route taken by Robert Campbell, a Hudson's Bay Company trader who, in 1840, became the first European to reach the upper Yukon watershed.

The Five Finger Rapids Debate
Klondike Highway, 14.5 miles (23 km) north of Carmacks

Five Finger Rapids, seen on the Yukon River from the highway turnout, received its name from the five channels, or fingers, created by four basalt pillars spaced more or less equally across the river channel. W.B. Moore, an early Yukon miner from Tombstone, Arizona, first used the name in 1882. The next year, Frederick Schwatka renamed the spot Rink Rapids after Danish geographer, Henry Rink. Miners, though, continued to use the name Five Finger, and George Dawson of the Geological Survey of Canada settled the matter by giving the name Five Finger Rapids official government sanction in 1887. Dawson then applied the name Rink Rapids to a smaller rapids downstream.

Fort Selkirk First Fur Post on Yukon River
Minto Resorts, Klondike Highway, Minto Landing, 44.5 miles (72 km) north of Carmacks

A riverboat tour operating out of Minto Resorts takes visitors 20 miles (32 km) downstream on the Yukon River to Fort Selkirk. With the exception of a government caretaker, no one lives at

Sternwheeler churning south through Five Finger Rapids.

Fort Selkirk today, but it was once home to several hundred people. Now, the only access to the old town is by boat or plane.

Robert Campbell founded Fort Selkirk when he established a trading post here for the Hudson's Bay Company in 1848. Campbell believed that the river downstream from his trading post was an extension of the Pelly, the river that brought him to the Yukon. The river upstream, on today's Yukon, Campbell called the Lewes.

In 1851 Campbell followed today's Yukon downstream as far as Fort Yukon in what is now Alaska. His journey established what many had suspected: that Campbell's Pelly River and the river that Hudson's Bay Company traders called the Yukon were actually the same river.

Fort Selkirk had been a trading center long before Campbell arrived in the area. The junction of the Yukon and Pelly had been a meeting place between members of the Northern Tutchone and Han tribes for hundreds of years. Chilkats, a Tlingit tribe from the coast, also came to this area to trade coastal goods and, later, European trade items such as guns, wool blankets, tea and tobacco.

After Campbell discovered the river connection with Fort Yukon, he arranged to receive trade goods through that post from Fort MacPherson via the Porcupine rather than from the south via the Liard River. This both reduced their cost and made them more readily available. It also immediately made the Hudson's Bay Company goods more competitive with Chilkat goods brought in from the coast. The new competition so angered the Chilkat that they attacked and pillaged Fort Selkirk. Campbell, with the help of two friendly Chilkat, had to run for his life. The Northern Tutchone Chief Hanan rescued the Hudson's Bay trader, and Campbell, following Indian custom, gave the chief his name in gratitude. Hanan's descendants still use the Campbell family name.

After his rescue Campbell set out by canoe for Fort Simpson in the Northwest Territories. From there he traveled on snowshoes through the autumn and winter of 1852 until he arrived in Minnesota. Then he went by horse to Illinois and by train to Montreal. By then it was April and Campbell had spent the spring trying to persuade officials of the Hudson's Bay Company to mount a raid against the Chilkat to reestablish his Yukon River trading post. The Hudson's Bay Company declined to take up the challenge, however, and it would be another 40 years before a new trading post was established at Fort Selkirk by the independent trader Arthur Harper. Campbell eventually left the Hudson's Bay Company to take up cattle ranching in Manitoba.

During the Klondike Gold Rush, several more stores opened at Fort Selkirk because of its strategic location on the Yukon. A North-West Mounted Police post was also established.

For a time in 1898, the Canadian government even considered making Fort Selkirk the capital of the newly created Yukon Territory.

The community survived for the first half of the 20th century, but in the early 1950s steamboat traffic was abandoned on the Yukon in favor of the new Whitehorse–Mayo and Dawson City roads. The one remaining store, the Hudson's Bay trading post, closed. People who had made their living supplying wood to the steamboat companies had to find other employment. Almost all residents of Fort Selkirk moved to communities on the new highway.

Today, many of the old homes and buildings constructed between the 1890s and 1940s still stand. Some of them have been refurbished by the Heritage Branch of the Yukon government while others sag and rot at the edge of the encroaching forest. The old Taylor and Drury store is still here, but only the concrete steps and foundation of the Hudson's Bay Company store can be found. There are a couple of churches, the old Royal Canadian Mounted Police post, the community school and two graveyards, one for whites, the other for Indians. Store houses, built on stilts to cache meat from dogs and wild animals, still guard some of the old cabins. Because the site is inaccessible by automobile, visitors are likely to find themselves eerily alone here at one of the Yukon's great ghost towns.

Steamboats Stop at Minto Landing
Minto Road, Klondike Highway, 1 mile (1.6 km) past Minto Resorts, then 1.25 miles (2 km) down Minto Road to the government campground

---

Only a government campground remains at the old steamboat stop of Minto Landing. The old settlement of Minto was also a roadhouse stop on the Dawson–Whitehorse stage road. Originally, an Indian settlement called *Kitl-ah-gon,* the old stopping point was named for Governor General Minto, who visited the Yukon in 1900. Many of the ex-residents of the abandoned Fort Selkirk settled in Minto during the 1950s, but they moved on to Pelly Crossing or other settlements within a short time. Some stories have it that ghosts haunt the old settlement. These ghosts, it is said, drove away the former residents.

Robert Campbell Follows Pelly River to Yukon

Klondike Highway at Pelly Crossing, 22 miles (35 km) north of Minto

The Pelly River, which crosses the Klondike Highway here, was named by Robert Campbell in 1840. Campbell, along with three companions—two Indian guides and another employee of the fur trade—arrived on the river after traveling up the Liard River from the Mackenzie into today's Yukon Territory. From its mouth on the Liard, Campbell poled up the Frances River, then crossed the continental divide to the Pelly. Although the Russians had already discovered the lower reaches of the Yukon River flowing into the Bering Sea at Norton Sound, Campbell was the first European trader on the upper Yukon watershed.

In the spring of 1843, along with eight other men, Campbell returned to the Pelly and followed it all the way to the Yukon River, which he called the Lewes. Here, Campbell encountered Tutchone Indians, who told him they had never before seen white men. These Indians also told Campbell of another tribe farther downriver who would kill and eat them. Campbell scoffed at the story, but his men refused to go farther. Unable to proceed alone, Campbell returned with his men over the route they had come.

500-Mile Journey from Stewart River Saves Miners

Stewart Crossing, Klondike Highway at the Stewart River Bridge, 34.5 miles (56 km) north of Pelly Crossing

The first trading post on the Stewart River was built at the river's mouth in 1885. This post, called Fort Nelson, was established by three of the Yukon's most prominent pioneers: Arthur Harper, Alfred Mayo and Jack McQuesten. McQuesten and Mayo had met about 20 years earlier in Alberta's Peace River Country, where both had been trappers, prospectors and occasional traders. They ran into Harper on their way to the Yukon River in 1871. Although Harper traveled separately, all three arrived on the northern river about the same time, coming into the country following the Porcupine to its mouth at Fort Yukon.

McQuesten built a trading post on the Yukon River he called Fort Reliance 6 miles (10 km) below the mouth of the Klondike

River in 1873. This post remained in operation until 1882, when gold strikes on the Fortymile River (40 miles/64 km below Fort Reliance), whose mouth lay on the Yukon, made it advantageous to move the post there. Then in 1885 gold finds on the Stewart River created a rush of miners to this area.

The following summer Mayo, McQuesten and Harper opened Fort Nelson at the mouth of the Stewart to supply the influx of miners in that area. Early that winter, though, coarse gold findings on the Fortymile, the river sometimes referred to as the Shitanda (a corruption of the aboriginal name). This sent a stampede of prospectors back down the Yukon to the original Fortymile townsite.

The stampede to Fortymile left the 50 or so miners at Stewart River with only minimal provisions. McQuesten had already left for San Francisco to get more trade goods, but Harper and Mayo were so short of supplies that they ran completely out of flour long before spring. By then they also realized that the new gold strike on the Fortymile was so big that hundreds of miners were likely to pour into the area as soon news got out and the ice was off the river. If that happened, there wouldn't be enough food in the territory to get everyone through the following winter. To avoid a famine Mayo and Harper knew they had to get word to McQuesten to bring in more supplies.

Of the 50 men at Stewart River that winter, only a steamboat man named Tom Williams and a young Indian guide volunteered to make the treacherous trip to the coast. Harper gave them a letter addressed to McQuesten that could be mailed from Juneau if the two men could make it over the Chilkoot Pass. Williams and his guide left in February 1887, traveling up the ice-covered Yukon, across Lake Laberge and up the chain of lakes leading to the pass. Before they'd reached the summit, they'd eaten all their food except for a few spoonfuls of frozen flour. With only 30 miles (48 km) left before they reached the coast, a blinding blizzard blocked their path at the top of the Chilkoot. For three days they huddled, shivering in a small hollow scraped in the snow.

By the time the blizzard let up enough for them to travel, their faces, fingers and feet were blackened with frostbite. Both were nearly dead from exhaustion and hunger, but the Indian hoisted Williams on his back and stumbled down the mountain pass. Eventually, Williams made it to Healy's trading post, where he died. Everyone crowded around demanding to know why the men had risked the tortuous 500-mile (805-km) journey from Stewart River at that time of year.

"Gold," the Indian said. Then he pulled a handful of dried beans from a barrel in the trading post and tossed them on Healy's counter. "All same, like this," he said.

Healy had the letter the men had carried forwarded to Juneau, where it was sent on to McQuesten in San Francisco on the next steamer going south. Starvation was averted at Fortymile the following winter. But nobody ever bothered to record who the Indian was, not even his name.

Miner Eats Bear with Bear's Own Teeth
Stewart Crossing, Klondike Highway at Stewart River Bridge, 34.5 miles (56 km) north of Pelly Crossing

At the time of the gold rush to Stewart River in 1885, miners in the Yukon Valley were a hardy independent group of frontiersmen. Only a few hundred men lived in the thousands of square miles of the upper Yukon Valley. Cut off from access to supplies from the outside world for most of the year, and limited by the great distances goods had to travel during the summer months, miners had to make due as much as possible with what they could obtain from the land. They often adopted Indian tools and clothing. Virtually no glass was available in the region, so river ice was often used to make cabin windows.

At least one ingenious Irish miner on the Yukon fashioned a pair of false teeth from the molars of a bear he shot near his cabin. Shaping holes for the bear's teeth in dental plates pounded from tin, he fashioned a homemade set of dentures. Then he proceeded to eat his winter supply of bear meat with the bear's own teeth.

Miners' Meeting Called to Settle Poison Beans Affair
Stewart Crossing, Klondike Highway, 34.5 miles (56 km) north of Pelly Crossing

Just as in many other parts of North America, miners settled along the Yukon River years before any official government presence was established. The law-and-order vacuum was, in this instance, filled by miners who administeried their own justice through the traditional institution of the miners' meeting. Anyone could call a miners' meeting for any reason. If a man was charged with a crime, a judge, or chairman, was elected to preside over the proceedings. Guilt or innocence, as well as any punishment handed out, was decided by majority rule.

For the most part, miners' meetings in the Yukon Valley, where crimes were rare, operated with at least as much wisdom and restraint as would generally be found in criminal courts. One miners' meeting at Fortymile, for instance, settled a feud between two miners threatening to have a duel. If either man was found dead, said the court, even after a fair fight, the other would be hung. The men decided against the shoot-out.

One of the earliest miners' meetings in the Yukon Valley was organized at Stewart River in the winter of 1886. A pair of miners charged a man named Leslie with trying to poison them. According to the two miners, Leslie had cooked them a pot of beans seasoned with strychnine. Earlier in the year, the man had promised them that he would take them to a rich gold deposit on the Stewart. Leslie had no money or provisions of his own, but he agreed to take the two men on as full partners in his gold mine if they would share their winter supply of food with him.

When Leslie brought the men to the Stewart, however, his diggings turned out to be worthless. That winter, fearing retribution from his disgruntled partners, he cooked up the poisoned pot of beans. He then left the deadly meal heating on the stove while he went visiting another cabin up the river. When his two partners came home, they dug into the beans, but became violently ill after eating only a small portion.

Both were fortunate enough to recover, and when they did they charged their former partner with attempted murder. Leslie was found guilty. Even though it was the dead of winter, he was banished from the Yukon Valley with enough food to get him to Dyea on the other side of the Chilkoot Pass. Despite the extreme cold, Leslie was forced to leave for the Alaskan coast the morning after his conviction. He eventually made it over the pass, explaining to new prospectors coming in that he had been forced to leave the Yukon because of an Indian uprising. The following spring the first wave of new miners arrived on the river expecting to have to fight off Indian attacks. Instead, they found Yukon Indians as peaceable as ever.

Silver Trail Follows Stewart River
Junction, Highway 11 and Klondike Highway

Yukon Highway 11, known as the Silver Trail, begins at the Klondike Highway on the north side of the Stewart River Bridge, then follows the Stewart River to Mayo and turns northeast to Elsa and Keno City. The town of Mayo, originally called Mayo Landing, was first surveyed in 1903, at the confluence of the Stewart and Mayo rivers. The low riverbanks on the Stewart here provided suitable places to dock and unload steamboats at a site as close to the Duncan Creek mines as the sternwheelers could travel.

It was silver, though, that made the area's fortune. Keno City, at the end of the road, is almost deserted now, but in the 1920s silver strikes on Keno Hill and other points nearby made Keno City a boomtown. For a time, United Keno Mine at nearby Elsa was the largest silver producer in the world.

Gustavesons Secretly Mine Gold
Duncan Creek Road, Keno City

Before the discovery of silver, the Stewart River region had been a relatively rich placer gold mining region. Gold discovered on the river in 1883 sparked the first rush of miners into the Yukon watershed. Even though this first gold rush on the Stewart ended in 1885, when most of the miners left on the stampede to the new diggings in the Fortymile District, the Stewart River developed a reputation in succeeding years as a grubstake river. It was a stream where a miner could pan out enough money to pay for a year's provisions if he had to, but one unlikely to make anyone rich.

In 1898 many of the miners who had come north during the Klondike Gold Rush stopped to prospect along the creeks of the Stewart River. The writer Jack London was one of these. So were three Swedish immigrants—a father and his two sons—named Gustaveson.

The Gustavesons found lucrative placer deposits on the then unnamed Duncan Creek, a tributary of the Mayo. In order to keep their find to themselves, and because their isolated location made them feel somewhat secure, they decided not to record their claim. They stayed on the creek, mined gold and erected a water-driven sawmill. Only occasionally did they venture into Dawson for supplies.

After a few such trips, however, other miners on the Klondike began to notice that the Gustavesons seemed exceedingly prosperous, sometimes spending hundreds of dollars while they were in town. In addition, the nuggets they spent in Dawson had a different color and shape than those found along the Klondike creeks. Rumors began to spread that the Gustavesons operated a rich secret mine. On several occasions men tried to follow the three men from Dawson on their return trips. But the three Swedes always managed to give their pursuers the slip before they reached the Stewart River.

Then in September 1901 four Dawson miners—Allan McIntosh, Colin Hamilton, Duncan Patterson and Jake Davidson—while camped on the McQuesten River, happened to see the three Swedes heading downstream on one of their trips to Dawson. They immediately suspected that the Gustavesons' secret mine was in the area, so they started poling upriver in the direction the Swedes had come from.

A few miles upstream they discovered a cache and what looked like a place where a boat had been launched. An uncertain trail led them for several more miles across the McQuesten Valley, then up another creek and finally to a canyon on today's Duncan Creek. Here, they found the Gustaveson mine. Quickly determining that none of the ground had been staked, the four men staked out claims of their own. They named the stream Duncan Creek after Duncan Patterson, who staked the discovery claim.

As soon as the four recorded their claims in Dawson, word spread and a stampede to Duncan Creek began. By 1902 Duncan Creek was staked from its headwaters to the Mayo River. Cabins were built on almost every claim and a wagon road led from the creek all the way to the mouth of the Mayo on the Stewart River. The Gustavesons left the country, returning to Sweden, and as far as anyone knows, they never returned. At the time it was estimated that they took at least $30,000 in gold with them when they departed, an amount worth about $500,000 in today's dollars.

Keno Hill Silver Expensive to Transport

Keno City, Silver Trail, 69 miles (111 km) northeast of Klondike Highway

Silver was first discovered in the Keno area, near the end of today's Silver Trail, at Galena Creek by J.A. Davidson in 1903. A decade later this deposit (known as the Silver King) was producing so well that additional prospecting and staking began. Then in 1919 Louis Bouvette discovered a rich silver deposit on what had been known as Sheep Hill but was soon renamed Keno after Bouvette's mine. Bouvette had named it after a game of chance popular then with miners all over the West and North.

By 1920 Keno City had become a boomtown. Six hundred claims had been staked on and around Keno Hill. The Silver King had already produced more than 2,500 tons (2,270 tonnes) of high-grade ore by the time the new claims began producing. But the expense of shipping the silver–lead ore to the smelter in San Francisco was great. The ore went by sternwheeler down the Stewart River and up the Yukon to Whitehorse. From Whitehorse the White Pass & Yukon Route railway took it over the mountains to the port of Skagway and tidewater. Here, the ore was shipped by boat to San Francisco.

Despite the long route, getting the ore over the relatively short distance on horse-drawn sleigh from Keno City to Mayo on the first leg of the journey was the most expensive part of the trip. In fact, transportation on that portion of the route cost the mines about the same amount of money as it did for them to get the ore from Mayo all the way to San Francisco. Once a good road was built between Keno and Mayo, the cost was reduced by approximately 60 percent. Later, costs were further reduced when bulldozers replaced horses on the route. Then in 1950 a road from Mayo to Whitehorse made it possible to truck ore directly to the railroad. This not only reduced costs significantly, but also allowed the ore to be shipped in any season instead of only in the summer months, when the ice was off the river. Today, of course, goods from the Yukon can be trucked on the highway all the way to Skagway or sent south on the Alaska or Cassiar highways.

Old Dance Hall Becomes Keno City Museum
Keno City, Silver Trail, 69 miles (111 km) northeast of Klondike Highway

The Keno City Museum is located at the end of the Silver Trail in Keno City. Nearby mining camps once made this area the largest silver producer in North America. Housed in an old dance hall, the museum features exhibits of the area's gold and silver mining as well as early community life. A brochure outlining an historical walking tour of Keno City is available. Hiking any of the several trails in the hills surrounding Keno City is also of historical interest. Old cabins and mines as well as an old tramline can be seen on some of the trails. The summit trail can be driven.

Robert Campbell's Assistant Discovers Stewart River
Klondike Highway, 10 miles (16 km) north of Stewart Crossing

James Stewart discovered the Stewart River in the winter of 1849. Stewart worked as Robert Campbell's clerk at Fort Selkirk and traveled down the Yukon River that winter to look for a party of Indians. On his quest, he traveled farther north on the river than any Hudson's Bay man had ever gone. When he returned, telling of the large river joining the Yukon, Campbell gave the new river Stewart's name. In 1852, when Chilkat Indians sacked Fort Selkirk, Stewart was away picking up supplies at Fort Yukon. When he returned he found Campbell with the northern Tutchone Chief Hanan. Campbell took two men and left for Fort Simpson. Stewart escaped back downriver to Fort Yukon with six other Hudson's Bay Company employees.

Tintina Trench Crosses Yukon and Alaska
Klondike Highway, 75 miles (121 km) north of Stewart Crossing

Part of the Tintina Trench, a large geological fault line that runs through much of interior Alaska and the Yukon, can be seen from the roadside near a highway marker here. The trench forms a long gap in the mountains, sometimes as much as 15 miles (24 km) wide, that was first noted in 1902 by R.G. McConnell of the

Geological Survey of Canada. He named this huge, spruce-covered valley *Tin-tin-a,* a word he thought approximated the Northern Tutchone word for "chief."

During the last ice age, the Tintina Trench, along with most of the course of the Yukon River and much of the interior of Alaska and the Yukon, lay in a semi-arid, ice-free zone now called Beringia. At the time, much of the world's water was frozen, causing the shoreline of the Bering Sea to retreat and create a land bridge between North America and Asia. North America's first residents used the bridge to cross over to this continent.

In the mythology of Alaska's and Yukon's first peoples, the land was once covered with water. When the water receded, a hero figure called Traveler changed the giant man-eating creatures of early times into the animals we see in the North today. Scientific data collected about the Beringian subcontinent supports the existence of giant animals like the legendary creatures of aboriginal myth. According to scientists, in addition to being home to North America's first people, some of the world's last giant creatures roamed this ancient land. These Beringian animals included the woolly mammoth, standing 10 feet (3M) at the shoulder and weighing as much as 3.5 tons (3.2 tonnes); the American lion, one of the largest flesh-eating animals to live during the ice-age; the American mastodon, a slightly smaller version of the woolly mammoth; the giant beaver, as large as today's black bear; and the scimitar cats, about the size of a modern lion. Oversized ground sloth, steppe bison and North American short-faced bear also roamed this northern land.

Half a Million Head for Klondike
Klondike Highway, 83.5 miles (134 km) north of Stewart Crossing

---

The highway follows the Klondike River from here to its mouth at Dawson City. The discovery of gold on tributaries of the Klondike sparked the great Klondike Gold Rush of 1897–98. Although other gold rushes have unearthed larger quantities of gold, the Klondike produced some of the richest individual claims ever made, and one creek, the Eldorado, became the richest gold placer mining creek in history.

One pan taken from the Eldorado in the fall of 1896 reportedly paid $1000. Several pans reportedly paid hundreds of dollars and eventually every claim on the creek, from Claim 1 to Claim 40 above discovery, would earn at least half a million dollars. Of course, no one knew this when staking a claim. The creek was, as yet, untried, and in many ways staking a claim was like buying a lottery ticket.

Many disappointed fortune seekers sold their claims for a few thousand dollars only to discover that the new owners had struck it rich. One pair of prospectors, Al Thayer and Winfield Oler, after a cursory examination of their claim at #29 Eldorado, concluded the ground there was worthless, so they returned to Fortymile and unloaded their claim on Charley Anderson, soon to be known as the Lucky Swede. Anderson was drunk when he bought the claim from Thayer and Oler for $800. When he sobered up Anderson first went to the Mounted Police to see if they would get him his money back—they wouldn't—Anderson left for the creek where his new claim eventually yielded more than a million dollars.

Even with such spectacular fortunes being made, the most incredible aspect of the Klondike Gold Rush was the tremendous prolonged excitement it created in people throughout the world and the remarkable journey that had to be undertaken by those who actually joined the rush. No one knows how many people attempted to take part in the stampede, but estimates run as high 500,000. Most would-be gold seekers, however, never got within a thousand miles of the place. Of those who did, no more than 50,000 of them actually made it to Dawson, and of these, less than half even bothered to look for gold. Some turned around immediately and started for home. Most of the good claims had been staked by 1897 anyway, and for the majority of suffering argonauts, just getting to the Klondike had become what mattered. The men and women who came to the Klondike in 1897–98 had become part of a spectacular historical event, and for many, whether they found gold or not, their journey there became the greatest single episode of their lives. Will Langille, who never found any gold, probably summed up the feelings of his fellow stampeders when he said he "would not have missed it for anything."

Sergeant Dempster Finds Lost Patrol
*Dempster Highway Junction, Klondike Highway, 87 miles (140 km)
north of Stewart Crossing, 25 miles (40 km) east of Dawson City*

The Dempster Highway leads north from this point to Inuvik on the Mackenzie River Delta. Initially, the road follows the spruce-covered valley of the North Klondike River. As the road continues, it crosses the continental divide between the Yukon and Mackenzie River watersheds, gradually rising above the treeline as it moves into the open hills, mountains and tundra of the Yukon Arctic. Across the Yukon line, in the Northwest Territories, the highway enters the Mackenzie River Delta and finally terminates at Inuvik, near the shores of the Beaufort Sea, as far north as you can drive in Canada.

In the early days of the Yukon, the North-West Mounted Police patrolled the route between Dawson City and Fort MacPherson (south of Inuvik on the Mackenzie Delta), by dog sled. Today's highway is named for Inspector Jack Dempster, who covered the route several times and also led the party that found the remains of Inspector Francis Fitzgerald's now famous Lost Patrol.

Fitzgerald set out with his four-man patrol from Fort McPherson with constables Sam Carter, George Kinney and Richard Taylor four days before Christmas in 1910. Normally, the Dawson–McPherson patrols originated in Dawson City. This time, though, because of available manpower, the 950-mile (1,529-km) round trip started at McPherson. In the end the northern starting point of the patrol probably had more to do with its ultimate disaster than any other single cause.

Supplies were not as plentiful at Fort McPherson as at the larger and better-stocked Dawson City. This meant the Fitzgerald patrol set out with provisions high in carbohydrates and low in protein and fat—two crucial ingredients in the diet of human beings facing daily temperatures dipping to –40° and –50° or even colder. The patrol probably hoped to supplement their diet with game killed along the way. But hunting during the winter season was always chancy, and as things turned out, no additional food was to be found, which made starving and freezing to death real threats.

Snowstorms and cold temperatures on the patrol's first days on the trail put the Fitzgerald party well behind schedule by the time they reached the Peel River. Within a few more days, it became increasingly obvious that their allotment of food wouldn't be enough to get them to Dawson. Still they held out hope for finding game along the way.

Twenty-one days into the journey, fate delivered what would prove to be its most severe blow. Fitzgerald and his men somehow passed by the Forrest Creek turnoff on the Little Wind River. The next few days were wasted going up and down the trail, looking for the missed stream.

Finally, with only four days' food left, Fitzgerald decided to turn his party around and return to Fort McPherson. He almost made it, but in the end, four days' worth of food, even when supplemented with meat from killing and eating their dogs, would not be enough. Two of Fitzgerald's patrol died of starvation and exposure only 35 miles (56 km) from Fort McPherson. Fitzgerald and another man pushed on for another 10 miles (16 km) before they, too, succumbed.

At the end of February, Corporal Jack Dempster was sent from Dawson City to look for the lost patrol. By mid-March Dempster had found traces of several of Fitzgerald's camps on Little Wind River, all within a few miles of each other. The proximity of the camps where Fitzgerald's men had wasted several days looking for the Forrest Creek Trail suggested to Dempster that they had become lost.

After determining that the patrol had turned back here, Dempster pushed on toward Fort McPherson. On the Seven Mile Portage, as he neared the fort, he found the bodies of George Kinney and Richard Taylor, along with a pot filled with cut-up rawhide, evidently used in an attempt to make a rawhide stew. The next day only 25 miles (40 km) from Fort McPherson, he found the bodies of Sam Carter and Inspector Fitzgerald. A note from Fitzgerald, found on his body, asked that his money be sent to his mother in Halifax, Nova Scotia.

Bishop Eats His Boots
Dempster Highway Junction, Klondike Highway

A near-tragic northern scene in the area near the Dempster Highway later became the inspiration for Charlie Chaplin's famous scene in the movie *The Gold Rush*. In the movie Chaplin eats his boots to keep from starving.

In the 1890s, in real life, northern missionary Bishop Stringer, while lost in an ice fog at –40°, hit on the idea of making soup from his and his companion's seal skin and walrus-soled boots when they ran out of other provisions. The boots were boiled for seven hours, after which, according to the Bishop, they were still tough and stringy although the broth was "fairly satisfying." Eventually, the Bishop found his way to a native village near the Arctic Circle, close to Eagle Plains on today's Dempster Highway. He had lost 50 pounds (23 kilograms) but was nursed back to health by Indians at the village.

Claims at Hunker Creek Bear Gold
Klondike Highway, 17 miles (27 km) west of Dempster Highway

Hunker Creek, a small tributary of the Klondike River, was staked soon after gold was discovered on other tributaries of the river in 1896. George Carmack's discovery on August 17 of that year brought miners to the area from up and down the Yukon River. Albert Hunker staked the first claim on his namesake creek on September 11. By the time word of the gold finds reached the outside world the following year, most of the creeks in the Klondike area had already been staked from their headwaters to their mouths. This provided no deterrent to the thousands of men and women who joined the Klondike Stampede to the Yukon in 1897–98.

Before Carmack's discovery sparked the stampede, miner Robert Henderson had been prospecting along the upper reaches of Hunker Creek. He called the stream Gold Bottom because he had found good prospects there, although he had made no major discoveries. It was Henderson, in fact, who invited George Carmack to prospect up the Klondike. Carmack and two companions, Tagish Indians Skookum Jim and Tagish Charlie, ventured down Hunker Creek to visit Henderson's claim, but they were more interested in exploring a nearby stream, now known as Bonanza.

Carmack's staking of the discovery claim on Bonanza sparked the Klondike Gold Rush, while Henderson continued mining just over the hill on today's Hunker Creek, unaware of what was happening nearby. Nobody from the Carmack party alerted him to their find—which the informal miners' code of the day called on them to do—because they had become angry at Henderson for his racist attitudes toward Skookum Jim and Tagish Charlie. Once other miners started pouring into the area, Henderson even lost his opportunity to stake a good claim on Hunker Creek. He was still working on the upper reaches of the stream, unaware of what was going on, when Albert Hunker staked his discovery claim far downstream. Before Henderson knew what was happening, other miners had staked much of the creek he had been working for weeks. Quickly, he staked a claim on Hunker's banks, but he eventually sold it for a few hundred dollars to obtain fare to California for medical attention. For the rest of his life Henderson searched for another Bonanza, but Hunker Creek was as close as he ever came.

Hydraulic Excavators Come to the Klondike
Bear Creek Historic Mining Camp, Klondike Highway, 17.5 miles (28 km) west of Dempster Highway

Bear Creek became the center of mining operations in the Klondike during the early years of the 20th century. The National Historic Sites branch of the Canadian Parks Service acquired the site in 1975. Guided tours are offered and many industrial artifacts of gold mining can be seen here—including the old "gold room" where gold was cleaned, melted down and cast into bullion.

Early miners in the Yukon used rudimentary tools compared to the industrial giants of later years. They panned gold by hand, used sluice boxes—12-foot- (4-M-) long wooden troughs that caught gold dust and nuggets in the wooden ribs spaced along the bottom as water poured through—or rockers, washing-machine-like contraptions that extracted gold from gravel as it was washed through a series of catch-floors from top to bottom. The gravel, which miners dug by hand from the bottoms of shafts with side tunnels along the pay streaks, was piled during the winter months near the sluice boxes. Once the spring melt came, miners shoveled the gravel into the sluice boxes and rockers, where the runoff water from the creeks washed out the gold.

Methods of the early miners were primitive, but that's what made individual placer mining attractive. Anyone could mine placer gold without the huge amounts of capital normally required for hard-rock mining. After the placer miners had skimmed the cream from their Klondike River claims, industrial mining came to the Yukon. Once that happened far more gold was extracted from the Klondike than any of the original miners could have dreamed possible.

Dredges arrived in the Klondike in 1904, and they worked here continually until 1966. Today, placer gold mining continues in the Klondike, although now with the customized efficiency of modern bulldozers, hydraulic excavators, conveyor systems and large-volume dump trucks. More sophisticated sluice systems recover more gold now than would have been possible at the turn of the century.

Yukon Ditch Dredged through Gold Fields
Klondike Highway, 18 miles (29 km) west of Dempster Highway

Huge gold dredges scoured the Klondike River valleys from soon after the turn of the century until 1966. Additional information about gold dredging can be found at Parks Canada's Dredge #4, a reconditioned dredge with guided tours 8 miles (13 km) south of the Klondike Highway on Bonanza Creek Road.

Belinda Mulroney Starts Town of Grand Forks
Klondike Gold Fields, 23 miles (37 km) west of Dempster Highway on Klondike Highway and 10 miles (16 km) south on Bonanza Creek Road

On Bonanza Creek, prospectors George Carmack, Skookum Jim and Tagish Charlie made the spectacular gold strike that sparked the start of the Klondike Gold Rush of 1897–98. On August 17, 1896, the day of their discovery, everything changed in the Yukon. Within two years of their find, the Indian fish camp at the mouth of the Klondike River would become part of the largest city in North America west of Chicago and north of Seattle. Miners would suddenly be able to buy Paris fashions, exotic foods and southern household goods in the new city of Dawson.

But Dawson wouldn't be the only new community in the Klondike. Out on the creeks near where Carmack and his companions first discovered gold, another new town called Grand Forks would sprout almost as quickly. This new town would develop around a hotel built in 1897 by 27-year-old Belinda Mulroney. Dawson businessmen warned Mulroney that Dawson City was the only sensible place to build, but she decided to construct her hotel in the heart of the gold fields near the forks of the two richest creeks, Bonanza and Eldorado.

A departing stagecoach in front of the Empire Hotel in Dawson City.

Mulroney came from Pennsylvania, but she had worked for several years on the Pacific Coast Steamship Company's *City of Topeka*. Her ship was servicing centers along the Alaska Panhandle when word first reached the outside world of the gold discovery on Bonanza Creek. Taking advantage of her proximity to the gold fields, Mulroney bought $5,000 worth of cotton goods and hot water bottles from money she had earned trading furs with Indians. She then freighted her goods over the Chilkoot Pass. At Lake Bennett, she hired on as a cook for a group of miners heading to Dawson in exchange for having her supplies hauled along with them.

Once in Dawson, Mulroney took her last 50-cent piece and

threw it into the Yukon River, vowing never to need small change again. She then took her $5,000 cache of cotton and hot water bottles, and peddled them in supply-starved Dawson City for more than $30,000. Mulroney had originally planned to start a restaurant with the profits but decided Dawson had too many restaurants already. Instead she used her money to build a hotel close to the mines.

Mulroney called her hotel the Grand Forks, and the town that grew up around it took the same name. By late 1898 ten thousand people called Grand Forks home, and Belinda Mulroney owned or had sold much of the local real estate. She worked behind the bar in her hotel, serving meals at half the cost of those in Dawson, but liquor at double the price.

Mulroney was known as a quiet person, never talking much but always listening to what the miners had to say. She regularly made wise mining investments that she first learned about while listening in on the gossip circulating in her hotel or after being given tips by the miners who stayed there.

As her earnings grew, Mulroney bought one of the prime business lots in Dawson and supervised the building of the what became the finest hotel in town. The Fairview had 30 private steam-heated rooms and a dining room with linen tablecloths, bone china dishes and sterling silverware. Cut-glass chandeliers decorated the lobby, and an orchestra played chamber music during supper hours. The night the Fairview opened it took in $6,000 and continued to make money for Mulroney until it was wiped out in the fire that destroyed much of Dawson in 1899.

During the winter of 1897, when food was short in Dawson, Mulroney went into partnership with Big Alex McDonald to buy supplies loaded in a small boat that had gone aground on a sandbar in the Yukon River. McDonald moved fast, rounding up all the flour and food that hadn't been ruined by the water. Mulroney was left with a few cases of whiskey and several crates of gum boots. Angry, but saying only that she would make McDonald regret his actions, Mulroney stowed away the gum boots and waited for the spring melt. When McDonald, the largest claim holder in the Klondike, came to her looking for gum boots for the dozens of miners he employed, Mulroney sold them to him for $100 a pair.

In the summer of 1900, champagne salesman Charles Eugene Carbonneau, who had been a barber in Montreal, arrived in Dawson City, claiming to be a French count. He courted Mulroney and sent her red roses every day throughout the summer. That autumn she agreed to marry him.

After the marriage Mulroney continued her business activities and soon became the first woman mine manager in the Yukon. Within a few more years she and the count went on to Fairbanks during the Tanana mining boom there. They left the North for good in 1910 after buying a ranch in Washington State.

Instead of retiring to the ranch, though, Mulroney and Count Carbonneau spent most of their time in Europe. The count convinced Mulroney to invest her money in a European steamship company, which went bankrupt soon after the outbreak of World War I. Then Count Carbonneau was killed, somewhat mysteriously, on a visit to the front lines. Mulroney returned to Washington State, living first on the ranch, then selling out and moving to the Seattle area, where she died in 1967.

Dawson City Built at Mouth of Klondike
Klondike River Bridge, Klondike Highway, 23 miles (37 km) west of Dempster Highway

---

Soon after gold was discovered on Bonanza Creek, prospectors began moving to the Klondike from up and down the Yukon Valley. One of these was Joe Ladue. But Ladue, who had been operating a trading post with Arthur Harper at the mouth of the Sixtymile River south of the Klondike, came looking for real estate, not a gold mine. While the first prospectors hurried to Bonanza Creek after the initial find, Ladue set out to get Klondike gold in another manner. He staked out a 160-acre (65-ha) concession at the mouth of the river and hurried to Fortymile to register his claim with the Canadian government.

Back on the Klondike, Ladue brought in a sawmill, built a warehouse and a small log saloon—which also served as his home—and started laying out streets. He named his new "town" Dawson City after the famous government geologist George M. Dawson. The first town lots he sold for five dollars each. By the following year, as the gold rush boomed, land prices escalated accordingly. By 1898, when the majority of the stampeders arrived in Dawson, town lots sold for several thousand dollars. Ladue became a millionaire.

Three miners work by candlelight in a mine on Gold Hill near Bonanza Creek.

Dubbed the mayor of Dawson, and famous throughout North America, Ladue returned in the fall of 1897 to his hometown in New York State. There he married his lifelong sweetheart, Anna Mason. Before he became rich and famous, Mason's father had scorned Ladue as a ne'er-do-well and had refused him permission to marry his daughter. Determined to make good, Ladue left New York State for the gold fields of the West. When Ladue returned from the Yukon, he was welcomed into the family with open arms. The 13 years Ladue had spent in the North had taken their toll, however. Despite his new wealth and recent marriage, he suffered miserably from tuberculosis. Little more than a year after his return, the disease killed him.

Mabel LaRose Holds Auction in Dawson
Dawson City

Dawson City grew in spectacular fashion after its founder, Joe Ladue, began laying out streets and selling lots. In the winter of 1896–97 only prospectors from the Yukon Valley itself were able to make their way to the new community, and lacking supplies from outside, many felt there would not be enough food to see the population through the long months of cold. Although the miners had struck it rich, there was nowhere to spend their money. They lived in crowded shacks on little more than bacon, flapjacks and biscuits until the following summer, when the ice went out of the river and sternwheelers could once again bring supplies to the upper Yukon from the world outside.

Stampeders on the Yukon River bound for Dawson in 1898.

With navigation on the Yukon open once more, word of the rich Klondike strike finally reached southern Canada and the United States. Within weeks the first of the stampeders began to arrive. In addition to miners coming in from the Alaska Panhandle, the new arrivals included merchants from the Northwest, doctors, lawyers, dance-hall girls, gamblers, musicians and all manner of others—each equally intent on getting rich. By the time the winter of 1897–98 set in, the new metropolis of Dawson sported a carnival-like atmosphere fueled by gold, where every second door on Front Street opened into a saloon, dance hall or gambling joint.

That winter, one of the dance-hall girls, French Canadian Mabel LaRose, decided on a novel way to make money and find winter accommodations. She climbed up on the bar in the Monte Carlo and auctioned herself to the highest bidder, agreeing to do housekeeping and act in every way as a miner's wife until spring breakup. There were a few stipulations: the money had to be held by a neutral party until spring, and LaRose had to like the looks of whoever won the bidding. LaRose made $5,000 on her auction. A few months later another dance-hall girl agreed to marry a wealthy miner in exchange for her weight in gold, an amount that, despite her diminutive size, brought her more than $25,000.

A group of Dawson prostitutes outside their places of business in 1898.

In Dawson City dance halls, miners paid a dollar a dance to spend their evenings in the company of the young women employed there. The women earned a percentage of the money their clients spent at the bar, but many were expert at taking their customers for much more. One of the best, Gertie Lovejoy, or Diamond Tooth Gertie as she was known to Dawson residents, once said of the miners and their gold that "the poor ginks have just gotta spend it, they're that scared they might die before they have it all out of the ground."

The fate of Dawson's dance-hall girls often contrasted sharply with that of the women of the nearby red-light district, where suicides, drug addiction and slavery were common. Many of the dance-hall girls left the Klondike wealthy women, while most of the miners from even the richest claims ended their days as poor as they'd been before the gold rush began.

Diamond Tooth Gertie One of Many Dawson Nicknames
Diamond Tooth Gertie's Gambling Hall, Dawson City

Diamond Tooth Gertie is remembered today primarily because of Diamond Tooth Gertie's Gambling Hall in Dawson. Sponsored by the Klondike Visitors Association, Gertie's has operated out of Dawson's refurbished Arctic Brotherhood Hall since 1971.

The real Gertie was a prominent Dawsonite during the gold rush era although she never owned her own gambling hall. Her real name was Gertie Lovejoy, but everybody called her Diamond Tooth Gertie because she wore a diamond fastened between her two front teeth.

In Dawson half the population went by a nickname of one kind or another. Other women in town sported names such as Sweet Marie, Klondike Kate and the Oregon Mare. There were also dozens of "Kid" sobriquets used in Gold Rush Dawson—the Wake-Up Kid, the Kansas City Kid, the Arkansas Kid, the No Shirt Kid and the Flap-Jack Kid to name just a few.

Several different men—George Carmack, Big Alex McDonald, Swiftwater Bill Gates and others—each claimed the title King of the Klondike. Gates went so far as to pay bellboys in his Seattle hotel to point him out to other guests as the King of the Klondike.

Swiftwater Bill—Raconteur and Bigamist
Front Street, Dawson City

Swiftwater Bill Gates got his nickname because of his tendency in the days before the gold rush to tell tall stories about his former prowess as a boatman on the Coeur d'Alene River in Idaho. When gold was discovered on the Klondike, Gates was working as a dishwasher in Circle City across the boundary in Alaska. Of all the miners in the log cabin town, none appeared less likely to become king of anything than Bill Gates.

Gates was a diminutive 5'6" (168 cm), hustling jobs and chances where he could find them in Circle City. When he arrived on the Klondike early in 1897, he and six other men went to work on a lay, or lease, at #13 Eldorado, agreeing to pay the owner of the claim half of whatever gold they dug from the ground over the season.

Most of the miners had shunned #13 because of their superstitious natures. But the seven men who went to work at the claim soon discovered there was nothing unlucky at #13 Eldorado. It soon became obvious that the diggings would bear a fortune in gold when cleanup came in the spring. Keeping the news to themselves, however, the seven men quietly spread the rumor that sample washes were only bringing 10 cents to the pan. Meanwhile, the owner offered to sell his apparently lackluster claim to the men for $45,000, a price the new owners were able to dig from the claim in just six weeks.

With money in his pocket, Gates was transformed from diminutive braggart to wealthy mining magnate. He donned a Prince Albert Coat, top hat and the only starched collar in Dawson. Not being content just to spend his money as it came out of the ground, he borrowed more to buy partnerships in other mining properties and even part ownership in a new saloon and gambling hall called the Monte Carlo. Gates spent lavishly everywhere he went, gambling away huge sums—often several thousand dollars in a night—and he showered his favorite dance-hall girls with gold and gifts, particularly 19-year-old Gussie Lamore.

Once, after spotting Lamore having a breakfast of fried eggs—her favorite food—with another man in a local restaurant, Gates, in a fit of jealousy, bought every egg in Dawson, where eggs were constantly scarce. According to the legend, after waiting a couple of days for the egg crisis to build, he suddenly presented them to Lamore, an act that so delighted her she agreed to marry him later that year when he went to San Francisco to obtain furnishings and dance-hall girls for the Monte Carlo.

When Gates arrived in San Francisco, however, Lamore changed her mind—possibly because she was already married and had a three-year-old child. Undeterred, Gates married Lamore's younger sister Grace and bought her a big house in Oakland. The marriage lasted only three weeks, however, and immediately after the separation, Gates began wooing the youngest Lamore sister, Nellie. By then Gates was running out of money, and he still had to arrange for furnishings and dance-hall girls for the Monte Carlo.

Luck was on his side, in this case in the person of a California doctor named Wolf, who approached Gates looking for Klondike investments. Gates borrowed $20,000 from the good doctor, promising to pay 100 percent interest per year. With this new-found money he moved on to Seattle to make arrangements for the Monte Carlo. Here, he continued to make newspaper headlines, spending lavishly from his suite of hotel rooms, even ordering champagne for an effervescent bath before heading north.

When Gates arrived in Dawson, he found both Doctor Wolf and his Monte Carlo partner, Jack Smith, waiting for him. Wolf wanted his money back and Smith wanted reimbursement for the thousands of dollars in Monte Carlo money Gates had spent in San Francisco. Despite the huge sums, Gates managed to settle both claims against him by turning over his part-interest in the Monte Carlo to Smith and by digging into his mining profits for the rest. Afterward, almost without funds, he hurried off to London to raise additional money for a new mining venture.

Stopping in Seattle on his way home to the Klondike in the spring of 1899, Gates met Mrs. Iola Beebe and her two daughters, Bera, 15, and Blanche, 19. The widow Beebe wanted to invest in Klondike properties, but Gates, who was more interested in her daughters, spirited both girls off to a ship going north. Before they could make their getaway, however, Mrs. Beebe showed up to retrieve both girls.

A few weeks later, when Mrs. Beebe and her daughters arrived in Skagway, Gates was waiting on the dock to meet them. Somehow he regained the woman's confidence, and at the first opportunity betrayed it by running off to Dawson with her youngest daughter. They were married en route, and when Mrs. Beebe arrived in Dawson a few days later, Swiftwater persuaded her to invest her life savings in his latest mining scheme. Within the year her money was gone, while Swiftwater and Bera had left town, leaving her with their one-month-old daughter.

From Dawson, Swiftwater and his bride went to Nome, where he took on another lay claim and incredibly repeated his Klondike success on a smaller scale. Within a few weeks, however, he gambled his new fortune away at Nome's gambling tables. Leaving his bride, Swiftwater returned to Seattle and within a few weeks ran off with his 17-year-old stepniece, Kitty Brandon. Gates abandoned his new wife almost immediately, but by this time Mrs. Beebe had caught up with him again, looking for restitution.

Incredibly, Swiftwater talked her into financing another trip north, ostensibly to recoup her money. This time he went to the new gold rush town of Fairbanks, where he struck pay dirt on yet another lay claim. He made $75,000 on the deal, but before he could get out of town, both of his mothers-in-law showed up looking for a share of the money. He escaped Mrs. Brandon, who was also his sister, but Mrs. Beebe tracked him back to Seattle where she had him jailed for bigamy.

In the weeks that followed, Swiftwater quickly spent his latest fortune in lawyer fees and paying off his two mothers-in-law. He emerged from the deal nearly broke, but divorced from both of his wives. Ever the optimist he went back to mining, married several times more during his life, and finally died in 1935 while working a silver mine in Peru.

Dawson Booms in 1898
Front Street, Dawson City

The first rush of miners on the Klondike arrived soon after the Carmack party discovered gold on Bonanza Creek in 1896. But the world outside the Yukon Valley didn't learn of the strike until the summer of 1897. Although thousands left for the Klondike almost immediately, Dawson City was in such an isolated spot that only 6,000 people made it to the new mining town before winter closed all traffic on the Yukon River.

Over a million dollars in gold, ready for shipment to the U.S.
mint in San Francisco, stacked in front of a bank in Dawson City
during the summer of 1898.

After the ice left the river in May 1898, however, the main group of Klondike stampeders invaded the new town of Dawson. The first boats from the south—carrying stampeders forced to winter along the river when the Yukon froze the autumn before—arrived almost as soon as the ice was gone in the spring. During June, Dawson's population jumped from just over 6,000 to more than 30,000. Most of the additional stampeders had crossed the mountains over the Chilkoot and White passes, but new Dawson residents also began arriving on sternwheeled steamboats from St. Michael, 1,700 miles (2,736 km) away on the coast of the Bering Sea. These gold seekers, starting for the Klondike already in possession of more money than most argonauts, had first gone north on ocean steamers from West Coast cities such as Seattle or Victoria before transferring to river sternwheelers bound for the Klondike.

Seven thousand boats lined the Dawson waterfront during the summer of 1898. They tied up, one to another, several deep, on both sides of the Klondike. More were moored across the

Yukon in the even newer settlement of West Dawson. Corner lots on Front Street in Dawson, considered choice spots for saloons, sold for as high as $40,000. The two sawmills in town worked 24 hours a day. A brewery opened. The Masons and Odd Fellows each opened a hall. All manner of goods arrived on the same steamers that brought in stampeders. By the end of the year, Dawson, already the largest city in Canada west of Winnipeg, would have a telephone system, electric lights and moving picture shows.

Front Street on the Dawson City waterfront in 1898.

By the following summer, with more stampeders still arriving—some after two years on the trail—Dawson continued to boom, but its light was already beginning to fade for many would-be miners. For the vast majority of those who made the journey to Dawson, every worthwhile claim in the Klondike had been staked before they arrived. While the wealthiest of the miners and entrepreneurs of every variety spent lavishly in Dawson saloons and gambling halls, Front Street was alive with those who found no fortune in the Yukon. These men and women seemed to continually walk the crowded streets, looking for work or trying to sell their belongings to raise enough money to go home. So much gear was sold off by stampeders trying to raise the price of a ticket south that, for a time, flour sold for less in Dawson City than it did in Seattle.

Then in 1899 news of a new gold strike in Nome sent stampeders scurrying from Dawson to a new Eldorado. Dawson's day in the sun was over as quickly as it had begun. In the years immediately after the gold rush, Dawson remained an important mining center, but in the later years, it would almost turn into a ghost town. Eventually, tourists and higher gold prices would revitalize the town's economy. Never again, though, would Dawson City be able to claim its title as a major Canadian metropolis.

Stampeder Bicycles to Nome
Yukon River, Front Street, Dawson City

The rush to leave Dawson in 1899 for the new gold diggings in Nome saw stampeders crowding into the last sternwheelers of the season, and in the days after that, as the Yukon's short autumn turned into winter, men departed on foot and with sleds pulled by dogs. Undoubtedly, the most novel mode of transportation was adopted by a miner named Ed Jesson, who traveled most of the 2,000 miles (3,219 km) from Dawson to Nome on a bicycle.

Jesson had noticed the bicycle in the window of the Alaska Commercial Company store in Dawson. It cost him $150, but Jesson bought the bike, spent several days learning to ride it, then started out for the Bering Sea over the iced-over Yukon River. The day he left, the temperature was –20°F (–34°C). He made 50 miles (81 km) the first day, and since roadhouses were approximately 25 miles (40 km) apart all along the Yukon at that time, he decided he would be able to have a noon meal at his first stop every day, and get a room for the night at the second roadhouse, all the way to Nome. But things didn't work exactly the way he planned.

On his second day out, when the temperature fell to nearly –50°, the bike's rubber tires froze hard as steel, and the grease in the wheel bearings froze almost as hard. Fortunately, Jesson was able to hitch a ride on a dog sled into the Alaska community of Eagle. When the temperature warmed up a few days later, he set out again and made good time for several days. One day—over a smooth stretch of river ice with a tail wind—he made 50 miles (81 km) before noon. On another day he passed a prospector from Dawson who was ice-skating to Nome.

A few days after passing the skater, Jesson—pushed by an even stronger tail wind—crashed into a bank of ice along the river and broke the handlebar of his bicycle. Undeterred he fashioned a new handlebar from a spruce branch and started on. At Kaltag, where the Yukon meanders closest to the shores of Norton Sound on the Bering Sea, Jesson left the river and started peddling across the frozen tundra for Nome. For the final 200 miles (322 km), the first part over a rough trail, without roadhouses, his pace slowed considerably. But just a month after he left Dawson, Jesson arrived on the beaches at Nome, suffering from a temporary case of snow blindness but otherwise in good health.

Arizona Charlie Builds Palace Grand and Shoots Wife
Palace Grand Theatre, Dawson City

When Arizona Charlie Meadows arrived in Dawson in the summer of 1898, it didn't take him long to realize that the best gold mining around was in the saloons and gambling halls along Front Street. Meadows had once fought hand-to-hand with Geronimo. Later, he performed in Buffalo Bill's Wild West Show. Within four months after his arrival in Dawson, he had made a small fortune from a variety of businesses, including the publication of a souvenir newspaper glorifying the wealthiest Klondike miners.

In the autumn of 1898 Meadows began building the Palace Grand Theatre using lumber from the remains of two beached sternwheelers wrecked along the Yukon. The Palace Grand, which opened in July 1899, became the most elegant entertainment hall in Dawson. Meadows invited 40 people to attend a banquet in the hall on opening night, and each guest found a $100 bank note waiting on his or her plate.

Stage shows at the Palace Grand ranged from the popular theatrical productions of the day to shooting exhibitions by none other than Arizona Charlie himself. In these affairs—which always attracted sellout crowds—Meadows, dressed in familiar buckskin, would shoot at glass balls his wife held between her thumb and forefinger on the opposite side of the stage. One night Meadows missed, nicking the skin off one of his wife's fingers. No more shooting demonstrations were ever held at the Palace Grand.

After the turn of the century the Palace Grand changed hands several times. Then it served as a community hall in Dawson for several more years. Eventually, it was saved from destruction by the Klondike Visitors Association and donated to the Canadian government, which reconstructed the old building in 1962.

Gold Discovered at Palace Grand
Palace Grand Theatre, Dawson City

When construction crews refurbished the Palace Grand Theatre in the 1960s it was rumored that dirt, panned from under the floorboards, yielded thousands of dollars in gold dust dropped from the pockets and pokes of Klondike miners 60 years earlier. True or not, Dawson has a tradition of mining gold from unlikely places.

At the height of the gold rush, two children regularly panned the sawdust under the bar at the Monte Carlo and reportedly made $20 a day for their effort. During the depression of the 1930s, a few men in Dawson made a living panning the dirt from under the town's aging wooden sidewalks. Even as late as the 1940s, thousands of dollars in gold dust were recovered from the ruins of old saloons and dance halls. Fifteen hundred dollars was taken from under the Bank of Commerce by two men making repairs on the building. The manager of the Orpheum Theatre made $1,000 in one afternoon panning dirt from under floorboards being repaired there.

Jack London's Cabin Stands Here and in California Too
Jack London Interpretive Centre, 8th Avenue, Dawson City

Dozens of writers and soon-to-be-writers came north to report on the Klondike Gold Rush or became full-fledged participants in it, but none became more famous as a writer of Northern tales than Jack London. (Robert Service wouldn't arrive in the Klondike until several years after the gold rush). London left San Francisco for the gold fields almost as soon as word of the strike made its way south in July 1897. He was, in fact, one of the few stampeders who made it across the Chilkoot to the Yukon before the winter of 1897–98 closed the pass. London spent that winter in a cabin about 50 miles (80 km) from Dawson on Henderson Creek, a tributary of the Stewart River.

When a group of trappers found the cabin 50 years later, it was dismantled and moved to Stewart Island by Yukoners interested in preserving the history of the gold rush. Then in 1969 approximately half the logs were taken from Stewart Island to London Square in Oakland, California, by people attempting to reconstruct the building there. Before the entire cabin could be moved, however, the bottom logs were spirited away to Dawson City by Canadians who convinced the cabin should remain in the Yukon.

Today, both Dawson and Oakland boast replicas of Jack London's Yukon cabin, each with half the logs from the original building. In Dawson City, in addition to seeing London's cabin, visitors can look at a collection of photographs tracing London's journey to the Klondike and depicting some of the actual people whom London later turned into literary characters.

Robert Service Ducks Shot But Kills Dan McGrew
The Robert Service Cabin, 8th Avenue, Dawson City

Robert Service, the Bard of the Yukon, lived in a cabin in Dawson City from 1909 to 1912. During that time, he wrote *The Trail of '98,* a novel based on the gold rush, as well as *Ballads of Cheechako,* the last of his three volumes of poetry based on life in the Yukon. The Service cabin in Dawson probably dates from 1897 or 1898. The earliest official title to the property was held by Mathilda Day, beginning in 1900.

Although Service became known for his poetry about the Yukon, especially the Klondike Gold Rush, the poet didn't arrive in the territory until five years after the stampede had ended. At the height of the Klondike frenzy in 1897, Service had been a hobo, down on his luck, hitching rides on freight trains through California on his way to Mexico. It was only after the turn of the century that the young poet headed north, eventually landing a job in a bank on Vancouver Island. In 1904 he moved to White-horse to work for the Canadian Imperial Bank of Commerce. It was here that he wrote his first poem about the Yukon—a commissioned piece on Yukon history for a church program.

Years later, Service recalled that he really had no idea what his poem would be about. Remembering his promise, however, he wandered the streets of Whitehorse one Saturday night, trying to come up with something promising. He later said that as he walked he heard "sounds of revelry" coming from the various bars he passed and the line "A bunch of the boys were whooping it up" just popped into his mind.

Suddenly, Service had the first line for his poem, but he still didn't know what to write about. He decided to go to the bank where he worked. It would be a quiet place to compose a poem on a Saturday night. But Service had forgotten about the night guard. As he stumbled through the blackened doorway, the guard heard him coming and fired his pistol into the dark. Service heard the bullet whiz by his head. The guard had missed, but instantly Service knew that in a poem where a "bunch of the boys were whooping it up," a shooting, perhaps of Dan McGrew, was likely to follow. Of course, with a bout of poetic license, he immortalized his experiences:

> *A bunch of the boys were whooping it up in the Mala-mute Saloon;*
> *The kid that handles the music box was hitting a jag-time tune;*
> *Back of the bar, in a solo game, sat Dangerous Dan McGrew,*
> *And watching his luck was his light-o'-love, the lady that's known as Lou.*
>
> *When out of the night, which was fifty below, and into the din and glare,*
> *There stumbled a miner fresh from the creeks, dog-dirty and loaded for bear.*
> *He looked like a man with one foot in the grave and scarcely the strength of a louse,*
> *Yet, he titled a poke of dust on the bar and he called for drinks for the house.*
> *There was none that could place the stranger's face,*

though we searched ourselves for a clue;
But we drank to his health, and the last to drink was
Dangerous Dan McGrew.

In 1912 Service left his cabin in Dawson City, supposedly on one of his periodic trips to meet with publishers in Toronto and New York. This time, though, he failed to come back. Although Service always said that he would one day return to the Yukon, he never did. Instead, he spent most of the rest of his life in Europe, where he died in 1958.

Father Judge Starts Hospital
Father Judge Gravesite, Dawson City

Today on the north side of Dawson City, a simple cross next to a small white building marks the gravesite of Father William Judge, the Klondike's first missionary. Judge came to Alaska in 1884. He followed miners to Fortymile, then moved on to Circle City in 1896. Back in Fortymile that autumn, Judge heard about the big strike on the Klondike and so moved on with the stampeders to Dawson City.

Only Judge, of all the men hurrying to the new town, came for anything but gold. Loading his sled with medicines and supplies for a hospital instead of food for himself, he arrived looking gaunt and sickly. But he went to work building a church and hospital immediately.

When his first church burned to the ground, he cleaned up the mess and set to work building another. In his hospital, open to Catholic and Protestant alike, the priest worked, seemingly without sleep, at all hours of the day and night. Indeed, Judge gave up his sleeping quarters early in the hospital's history as stampeders, sick with typhoid and dysentery during the summer or scurvy in the winter, crowded his small building. Despite his frail health Father Judge literally ran from one job to the next.

In December 1898, the citizens threw a benefit for Father Judge, but life for the 45-year-old was running out. Years of deprivation and hard work had taken their toll, and on January 16, 1899, Father William Judge, whom many called the Conscience of the Klondike, died after a brief final illness.

Legends of Hollywood Dug Up in Dawson
Recreation Center, Dawson City

Entertainment in gold-rush Dawson tended to be on the wild and woolly side, but it included everything from sharp shooting and prize fights to dramatic presentations, concerts, can-can girls, gambling and evenings tripping the light fantastic with dance-hall girls. After the turn of the century, when the bulk of the stampeders had left for other places, entertainment in Dawson, for the most part, settled down to the same kind of activities that occupied citizens of small towns in other parts of North America. Foremost among them were the silent movies of the day.

In the early years of the century, though, movies sent north to Dawson City cost more to send back to the distributor in the south than they would cost to buy. Consequently, the only movies sent to Dawson were ones that had finished their runs in southern Canada and the United States. After they were shown in Dawson, no one ever bothered to send them back. Instead they were paid for and stored in the basement of Dawson's Carnegie Library building.

About 1929 this growing collection of old movies became too large for the library. Around the same time, the Dawson Amateur Athletic Association decided to fill in their swimming pool. Somebody figured it would be a good idea to use the old movies as part of the fill, so the film canisters were discarded and buried. Almost 50 years later, the town of Dawson started work on a new community center and was surprised to unearth 510 old movies, made between 1910 and 1925, including *Wild Fire* (1915) starring Lillian Russell and Samuel Goldwyn's first feature, *Polly at the Circus*. Because they were buried in permafrost, most were in good enough condition to be repaired, and many turned out to be the only copies still in existence.

Floods and Fires Plague Dawson
Front Street, Dawson City

When Joe Ladue staked out Dawson's townsite in 1896, his only concern was to make as much money as possible from his new town's strategic location at the mouth of the Klondike. The fact that the proposed village lay at a point along the Yukon River particularly prone to spring ice jams and flooding never bothered him for a moment.

Dawson City was built on a mud flat barely higher than the river, and the town's first flood occurred its first spring. The following year a major flood covered the new town as far back from the river as the North-West Mounted Police barracks. Several more small floods occurred after the turn of the century. Then in the spring of 1925 waters rose so high that people canoed through Dawson's streets.

Another major flood occurred in 1944 and several minor ones in the 1950s. Finally, in 1959 a dike was built to protect the town from future flooding. Unfortunately, even though the dike was upgraded in 1968, it still wasn't high enough to protect the town. In 1979 the worst flood in Dawson's history saw the Yukon River roll over the top of the dike and cover much of downtown Dawson, pushing many of its historic buildings off their foundations. Afterward a new larger dike was built, but even now there are no guarantees that the Yukon's waters have been tamed forever.

Fires have been responsible for almost as many catastrophes in Dawson's history as floods. The first major fire burned most of Front Street in November 1897. It was started, people said, when a dance-hall girl, Belle Mitchell, threw a lit lamp at a rival.

The following year the same woman left a candle burning on a block of wood and touched off a second fire. Once again, much of Dawson's business district was destroyed. This tragedy seemed harder to bear because the town's newly ordered firefighting equipment lay disassembled and useless in a Dawson warehouse at the time. The town, rich with gold, hadn't been able to come up with the $12,000 needed to complete the purchase.

As Dawson rebuilt in 1898, money was finally raised to pay for the fire-fighting equipment. A mostly volunteer fire department was also formed. But six months later the department's three paid employees went on strike for higher wages. As the strike progressed they let the boiler fires go out. Once again Dawson was without fire protection.

On the night of April 26, 1899, with the temperature a chilling −45°, the worst fire in the town's short history tore through Dawson. Fire fighters pumped water directly from a hole cut in the river ice, but it froze solid in the hoses before it could be sprayed on the fire. Even blowing up buildings in the fire's path didn't stop the blaze. By morning over 100 buildings in the center of Dawson had gone up in flames. Rebuilding the town began while the ruins of the old buildings were still smoldering.

Once more, new arrangements for fire fighting had to be made and later that year, a 20-member professional fire department was organized. But in January 1900 yet another $1 million fire raged along Front Street. One final great fire occurred in 1904, when all the buildings between Second and Third avenues were burned. This time, though, fire fighters saved Front Street.

Martha Black Elected to Parliament
Black's Residence, 5th Street, Dawson City

Martha Black came to Dawson City in 1898. Born to wealthy parents in Chicago, she and her husband, Will Purdy, a member of another prominent family, got caught up in the excitement of the Klondike when word spread of the discovery of gold here in 1897. When her husband got nervous and backed out of their plan to go north, however, Black left him, left her children with her parents and traveled north over the Chilkoot Pass with her brother instead. On the way she discovered she was pregnant again.

George and Martha Black stop for lunch on Yukon hunting trip.

The following January, alone at her cabin near Dawson, Black gave birth to her third son. By this time, however, she had already staked a mining claim. In the following years, Martha Black ran her own placer mining operation and also managed a sawmill in Dawson.

In 1904 she married George Black, a Dawson lawyer who was appointed Commissioner of the Yukon in 1912. In 1921 George was elected to the House of Commons. When he retired from public office in 1935, Martha, nearly 70 years old by then, ran for his seat and won. She was the first woman to be elected to parliament from the Yukon and the second woman to be elected to parliament in all Canada.

Last Run of the *Keno* Ends the Steamboat Era on the Yukon
Steamboat Keno, *Dawson City Waterfront*

More than 250 sternwheeled steamboats like the *Keno*, which now sits beached along Dawson City's waterfront, plied the waters of the Yukon River from the 1880s to the 1950s. Contracts for cord wood all along the river employed hundreds of people throughout the first half of this century. A trip from Whitehorse to Dawson City and back took, on average, 120 cords of wood—a cord of firewood for each hour of operation.

The trip, a distance of 500 miles (805 km), took 40 hours traveling downstream from Whitehorse, but the return from Dawson to Whitehorse going upstream took up to four days. Barges were often pushed ahead of the steamers.

Steamboats were used over the entire length of the Yukon River. Dawson received goods that came in from the south on the White Pass & Yukon Route railway from Whitehorse, and also goods from St. Michael, on Norton Sound, that had been shipped north by ocean liners and then transferred to the river sternwheelers.

The *Keno*, built in 1922, was used on the Mayo–Dawson City–Whitehorse run. Silver ore was stockpiled on the riverbank in Mayo all winter, waiting for the first trip of the *Keno* in mid-May. The *Keno* was used for ore transportation until 1948. From then until 1955, it was used for passenger and freight traffic on the Yukon. After an unsuccessful run as a tourist boat, the *Keno* ended its working days in 1959. Today the *Keno* is owned by Parks

Canada. Plans call for the old steamer to someday become a museum.

Dempster's Dog Bids Steamboats Good-Bye
Yukon River, Dawson City

Like other members of the North-West Mounted Police, Sergeant Jack Dempster, the man who found the Lost Patrol, spent a good part of his career carrying out his duties with dogs and sled. After he stopped making regular dog-sled patrols, he kept his lead dog as a house pet in Dawson City.

When Dempster and his family left the Yukon, the dog was given to another member of the force who took it with him to say good-bye when the Dempsters boarded a sternwheeler bound for Whitehorse. The dog barked as it watched the family go, and for the rest of its life, whenever any sternwheeler left the docks of Dawson, it would race to the waterfront and stand, howling, until the boat disappeared around the first bend in the Yukon River.

Whiskey Trader Invites North-West Mounted Police to Yukon
Yukon River, Dawson City

The ferry *George W. Black,* which docks at the end of Front Street on the north side of Dawson, takes passengers across the Yukon River to the starting point of the Top of the World Highway. This gravel road leads through the spectacular countryside of Fortymile River country, often well above the treeline as it passes over the rounded hills, sometimes with 360°-vistas, before it joins the Taylor Highway at Jack Wade Junction in Alaska.

The first North-West Mounted Police detachment in the Yukon was established at Fortymile in 1895. Although the place is a ghost town today, the old mining town—located 45 miles (72 km) downstream from Dawson at the mouth of the Fortymile River—was the largest settlement along the upper Yukon when the Mounted Police arrived in the territory. The force had been established 20 years before, in large part to quell the activities of American whiskey traders operating along today's Montana–Alberta border. The most notorious of these trading posts, Fort Whoop-Up, was owned by Montana trader John J. Healy.

Ironically, it was Healy, by then a trader at Fortymile, who first suggested to Sam Steele that the Mounted Police were needed to maintain Canadian law in the Yukon. Healy and his trading concern, the North American Transportation and Trading Company, had come into the region in the summer of 1893, challenging the long-held monopoly of the Alaska Commercial Company. The presence of competition on the upper Yukon lowered prices and made additional products available to the miners, but, while they welcomed the new store, they disliked the often cranky Healy for his unwillingness to extend credit.

Healy's troubles with the miners heated up when one of his employees called a miners' meeting—the extralegal institution that provided the only recourse to justice available in isolated mining areas beyond the reach of civil law—to redress a grievance she had with her employer. The employee, a woman hired as a housekeeper, was in the habit of staying out to all hours of the night and sometimes not returning until the following morning.

One night when she didn't return as ordered, Healy fired her and locked her out of the house. The miners' meeting voted the woman her salary for the year, plus free passage out of the Yukon the following spring. Healy paid up, but he wrote to his old friend Sam Steele and suggested the Mounted Police come to the Yukon. He also urged Church of England Missionary Bompas to make a similar request. It was Bompas's suggestion that more money than the cost of the force could be obtained by levying duties against American goods in the region that probably, more than anything else, spurred the government to send law to the Yukon.

In August 1894 Inspector Charles Constantine traveled to Fortymile to assess the situation for the Canadian government. He reported that a small detachment would not only maintain Canadian law but could also collect a substantial amount of revenue for the Canadian government in the form of excise taxes and import duties. The following year Constantine returned to Fortymile with a force of 20 constables.

The timing could not have been better. While communities on the upper Yukon were relatively free of crime in 1895 when the police arrived, gold discovered on Bonanza Creek the following summer would spark an invasion of the territory by thousands of stampeders from the south. Unlike the situation in neighboring Alaska, civil authority would already be firmly established in the Yukon by the time the gold rush stampeders arrived. As a consequence, much of the lawlessness that plagued the American territory during the gold rush of 1897–98 would be absent in the Yukon.

This is not to say that everything ran smoothly on the Canadian side of the international boundary. The Mounted Police were there to enforce the law, but along with the government presence came sometimes incredible instances of graft and corruption. Bribery appeared to be the order of the day at the mining recorder's office in Dawson. Names on claims were changed and lineups were long although those allowed through what was called the "five dollar door" came and went expediently.

Some miners who tried to file claims were told the ground was closed by government order, only to find out later that the property was being mined by friends of the recorder. The commissioner of the Yukon, ex-Mounted Policeman James Walsh, was also implicated in the corruption as were the Mounted Police themselves. In addition to their other duties, the police ran the postal services in Dawson. Here, it was said, a man's mail would be delivered quicker if he first crossed the appropriate palm with a few dollars in gold dust.

Chapter 2

The Alaska Highway

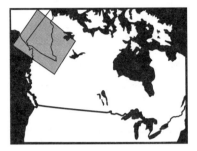

Dawson Creek to Fairbanks

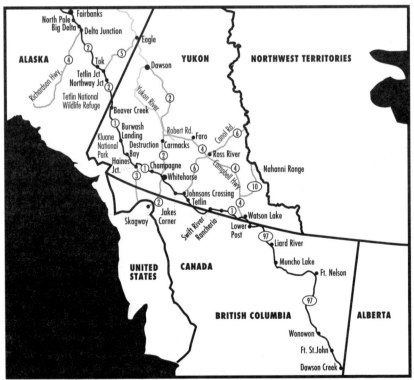

Travelers on the Alaska Highway almost always make a short stop at the beginning of the road in Dawson Creek, British Columbia, before they start the 1,500-mile (2,414-km) journey to Fairbanks. Most any summer day, visitors can be seen downtown, across from the Alaska Hotel, taking pictures of one another at the Mile Zero marker. Others come and go from the museum in the old Northern Alberta Railway station at the end of the street. All the while a steady stream of traffic—cars, trucks, campers and semitrailers—stop and go at the traffic lights along Alaska Avenue, the initial section of the great highway north.

A make-do carpentry shop at a construction camp on the Alaska Highway in 1942. The serviceman is Fred Ford of Strathmore, California.

Dawson Creek is a busy agricultural and commercial center today, but on December 7, 1941, when Japan bombed Pearl Harbor, Dawson Creek was a small, rather isolated farming community with only about 600 residents. The events half a world away soon brought the United States into World War II, however, and within three months the U.S. Army turned Dawson Creek into a supply center for one of the most ambitious construction projects ever undertaken.

At Pearl Harbor the Japanese destroyed most of the United States naval fleet in the Pacific. This, along with the lack of land-based defenses, left Alaska, the great American possession on the isolated northwest corner of the continent, unprotected and vulnerable to Japanese invasion. As the writer Jim Christy noted with only slight exaggeration, ground protection along the entire northwest coast of North America, from Vancouver to Nome, consisted of a cannon being used as a flower pot in front of the Capital Building in Juneau.

With the outbreak of the war, American officials quickly made plans to build a military road connecting Alaska with the rest of the United States. Because Dawson Creek lay at the end of the Northern Alberta Railway—at the northern terminus of the connected rail lines in North America—thousands of American troops soon began pouring into town with tons of equipment and supplies.

The American army had come north to build the Alaska Highway (originally named the Alcan) to link Dawson Creek and the system of roads in southern Canada with Fairbanks in the Alaska interior. A road to Alaska, no matter what route it took, would have to cross more than 1,000 miles (1,609 km) of muskeg, mountains, forests and permafrost through one of North America's few remaining large tracts of wilderness. But American military officials who planned the road were looking for more than just the easiest possible route across this northern expanse.

No route to Alaska would have been easy, but the most practical of the possible roads would probably have been the one the army called Plan A. It led along the eastern side of the Coast Mountains to Atlin, near the British Columbia–Yukon border and went on to Fairbanks from there. Some people thought this route too close to the coast and vulnerable to Japanese attack. Another proposed route, Plan B, followed the Rocky Mountain Trench north from Prince George, British Columbia, to Dawson City in the Yukon, then on to Fairbanks.

Military planners, however, soon chose a third route, called the Prairie Route. The beginning of this route lay far inland on the east side of the Rocky Mountains, far removed from any possible Japanese attack. Even more importantly, the completion of this plan would connect the system of airports already being built by the Canadian government on the Northwest Staging Route between Edmonton, Alberta, and Fairbanks, Alaska.

Military planners envisioned this string of air bases and the proposed highway as complementing each other. Each would be used to augment and supply the other. As well, additional airstrips could be constructed along the highway to beef up the effectiveness and safety of the Northwest Staging Route. Already aircraft were using the route to reach Alaska, the north Pacific and the Soviet Union.

Perhaps the most remarkable aspect of the construction of the original Alaska Highway was that it was completed in just eight months. Work began in March 1942, and the last link was finished at Beaver Creek, near the Alaska–Yukon border, in October of the same year. But speed came with a price. The Alcan pioneer road was barely serviceable. Much of it was only wide enough for one lane of traffic. Bridges were temporary structures built of logs. Corduroy roads—with trees cut from the forest and laid side by side on top of permafrost and muskeg bogs—stretched for miles on end. Treacherously steep road grades made driving many stretches of the Alcan seem like going over the big hump on a roller-coaster. And the continual twists and turns of the highway led to a rumor, believed by even some of the construction workers, that the road had been designed in this fashion to make truck convoys harder for the Japanese to bomb.

A convoy of trucks, including two bulldozers, pause at a muddy section of the Alaska Highway in 1942.

Despite its shortcomings, construction of the Alaska Highway was an incredible achievement. It required the concerted effort of two governments, 10,000 military personnel and several thousand civilians—as well as huge expenditures by the American government. Tons of supplies and equipment were required. The road the army built in 1942 was never meant to be anything but a pioneer road, a road that could get vital troop supplies north and then be used as a tote road in the building of an adequate year-round highway. Even before the army finished this pioneer road, civilian contractors were on the scene beginning the job of upgrading it to more reasonable standards.

Unlike the popular legend, building the Alaska Highway was not always a matter of cutting a new road through uncharted and uninhabited wilderness. Indeed, for much of the way, highway construction followed a series of Indian and fur-trade trails as well as a few primitive wagon roads. Upgrading and connecting these trails turned the old routes into a long single highway suitable for military vehicles. But the old routes were the real pioneer roads in the land between Dawson Creek and the Yukon River.

Both Indians and whites had lived and traveled throughout this region for years—for Indian people, thousands of years. Some of the first inhabitants of the Americas probably traveled south to settle the two continents on the same side of the Rockies as the southern portion of today's Alaska Highway. Europeans have a relatively short history in the area of the Alaska Highway, but they had lived, worked and explored the northern forests of the region for nearly 150 years before highway construction began.

George Dawson Gives Moniker to Frontier Town
Dawson Creek

Both Dawson Creek, British Columbia, and Dawson City, Yukon, were named after George Dawson, an early naturalist and government geologist in northwestern Canada. Frail throughout his life, Dawson was an unlikely outdoorsman. At 10 years old he suffered a crippling illness that arrested his physical development when he was still less than 5 feet (152 cm) tall. Schooled at home as a youngster he graduated from McGill University in Montreal and then attended the London School of Mines, where he graduated first in his class.

Back in Canada he joined the International Boundary Commission surveying the 49th Parallel between the Canadian and American West. As the expedition's geologist and botanist, Dawson supplied the British Museum with numerous specimens of animal and plant life of western North America. After the boundary survey was completed, the Canadian government appointed Dawson to the Geological and Natural History Survey of Canada.

This work took him from the Peace River country, in the area around today's Dawson Creek, as far north as the Yukon River. In addition to his reports on the geology, zoology and botany of northern and western Canada, Dawson's observations also included archaeological and ethnological information. His collection of northern artifacts helped develop the ethnological collection at the National Museum of Canada. In 1895 Dawson was appointed the Director of the Geological and Natural History Survey. He died six years later at the age of 51.

Only One Accurate Milepost on Alaska Highway
Mile Zero, Dawson Creek

The Mile Zero marker for the Alaska Highway—located in downtown Dawson Creek on the corner of 10th and 102nd streets—might be the only accurate milepost sign left on the Alaska Highway. Road improvements have been changing the Alcan's length ever since the original mileposts went up during the 1940s. Straightening twists and turns in the old road shortened the highway, and improving grades on the steepest inclines lengthened the road.

Overall, the highway today is more than 30 miles (48 km) shorter than it was when the mileposts first went up. This means that most of the lodges and stopping places that took their name from the original mileposts are no longer the distance they proclaim themselves to be from Dawson Creek. A few of the historical mileposts, based on the original mileposts, also remain on the highway, usually with details about the construction of the highway or other historical information on a plaque or signpost nearby.

To add to the confusion of the mileposts, Canada switched to metric measurements in the 1970s. Today, on the British Columbia portion of the highway, every five kilometers is marked by a kilometer post that notes the actual number of kilometers from Dawson Creek—as of 1990. In the Yukon there's a kilometer post every two kilometers, but the numbers reflect the metric conversions of the old highway mileposts—which, of course, are now wrong.

As a result kilometer posts in the Yukon do not correspond to those in British Columbia. The British Columbia–Yukon border, for instance, is at kilometer 967.6, according to the British Columbia signs, but at kilometer 1009 according to Yukon signs. If this isn't confusing enough, once you get to the Alaska border, mileposts once again appear. But the numbers are still the historical miles from Dawson Creek, which, of course, are inaccurate.

In this book, distances are based on actual miles driven, not the mileposts.

Fire Destroys Dawson Creek
Mile Zero, Dawson Creek

On February 13, 1943, a small fire broke out in a livery stable on Main Street in Dawson Creek. The American army turned out to fight the fire, and a large crowd gathered to watch. Neither the crowd nor the fire fighters knew that a construction company had stored a truckload of dynamite inside the building. Suddenly, as the crowd looked on, the building and several of the fire fighters virtually disappeared in a huge explosion.

The force of the explosion was so powerful that it was said to be felt six miles away. The vacuum it created was so great that one death was reportedly caused when a man standing near another building was sucked through a window. As many as twenty people were killed. While the area was still concealed in a cloud of dust and smoke from the explosion, flaming timbers rained down from the sky, setting other buildings in the area ablaze. An entire block of downtown Dawson Creek burned to the ground.

Once the blaze was put out, the army set up temporary mess tents for civilians and provided other aid to local people, including military police protection to guard the town against looters. Years later, one local man recalled finding a fifty-pound bag of sugar. Only a boy at the time, but knowing sugar's war-time value, he was struggling home with his booty when he heard the gruff voice of a military policeman behind him: "Where you all going with that boy?" After a lecture and a warning, the boy was sent home without his sugar. Rebuilding the downtown area began almost immediately after the fire.

Telephone and Teletype Lines Come to Alaska
Historic Milepost 2, 1.7 miles (2.7 km) from Dawson Creek

Along with the new road, the Alaska Highway brought several other major changes to the North, including a huge influx of people. In 1941 the area beyond Dawson Creek was even more sparsely populated than it is today. The population of the entire Yukon stood at less than 5,000. Alaska had a population of over 7,000, but most of these lived in coastal communities. The Alaskan interior was almost as empty as the Yukon, with the population's economy, outside the few major centers, resting on mining and fur trapping. A railroad ran between Seward and Fairbanks as well as between Skagway and Whitehorse, but life for most people, even in the major centers, was one of isolation from the outside world, little changed since the gold rush.

As much as a highway connection from the south, and with it the huge influx of people (more than 30,000 soldiers and civilians), life in many northern communities was also made less isolated because of the telephone and teletype lines that came from Edmonton along the highway. Almost overnight it became possible for people in communities all along the highway as well as in towns like Haines and Skagway, Alaska, and other communities off the highway to have telephone service to the outside world. With the highway, Cantel (Canadian Telephone) established one of the longest open-wire toll circuits in the world, opening an extensive network over 14,000 miles (22,530 km) long, using nearly 100,000 telephone poles. These days, of course, microwave towers handle the transmission of long-distance telephone calls across North America, including Alaska and Yukon, but at the time it was completed, the Cantel system brought modern communications into the North for the first time.

In addition to building the Alaska Highway and Cantel telephone system, the American army also undertook other related projects, some with long-term benefits for Alaska and the Yukon. These included the construction of building complexes along the Alaska Highway and the Canol Pipeline (bringing oil from Norman Wells, Northwest Territories to Whitehorse) and upgrading the White Pass & Yukon Route railway.

Telegraph Line to Connect Alaska and Siberia
Historic Milepost 2, 1.7 miles (2.7 km) from Dawson Creek

The Cantel system came about with the construction of the Alaska Highway, but the first attempt at bringing a communications line to Alaska began 80 years earlier. In the 1860s, while Alaska was still a Russian possession, the Western Union Telegraph Company planned a project to connect North America with Europe by a telegraph line crossing the 56-mile (90-km) Bering Strait between Alaska and Siberia. Several attempts to cross the Atlantic Ocean by cable had already been tried and each had failed. The telegraph company thought the chances of building a line across northern Canada to Alaska and Siberia held out more hope for success.

Work began simultaneously in British Columbia and Alaska. The British Columbia section started north on the east side of the Coast Mountains along a route that would later be considered for the Alaska Highway. In Alaska, Robert Kennicott, a naturalist from Northwestern University in Illinois, led a party undertaking the Alaska–Yukon section of the line. Arriving in St. Michael in August 1865, Kennicott split his force into two parties. One was to string wire to Nulato across the Seward Peninsula to the strait; the other larger group was to follow the Yukon River to its headwaters, laying a line that would meet the one coming north from British Columbia.

Progress turned out to be slow, and Kennicott, a scientist at heart, was not a good administrator. By the following May, when the main party had only reached Nulato, Kennicott suffered a heart attack and died. But the expedition pushed on under Kennicott's successor, chief surveyor Frank Ketchum. He and Michael Laberge explored the river that summer as far as the Hudson's Bay Company trading post at Fort Yukon, but wire crews lagged far behind mostly because they were short of sled dogs and Indian packers. Morale was low and often the entire expedition was short of supplies.

Early in 1867 Ketchum and Laberge explored the Yukon again, this time mapping the river far upstream into today's Yukon Territory. On Ketchum's return to St. Michael at the end of the summer, he discovered two important pieces of news. The first was that the United States had purchased the Alaskan territory from Russia. The second was that Cyrus Field had finally succeeded in his attempt to lay a transatlantic telegraph cable connecting North America and Europe. There was no longer any need for a telegraph line across Alaska, and the Western Union Telegraph Company canceled the project.

Last Remaining Timber Bridge Crosses Alaska Highway
Kiskatinaw Bridge, 17.3 miles (28 km) north of Dawson Creek

A short side trip takes visitors over a 2.5-mile (4-km) loop off the Alaska Highway along a section of the original road. In 1942 the United States Army Corps of Engineers cut a pioneer road for military traffic bound for Alaska, but the task of building a more permanent road fell to the civilian contractors who followed close behind (in several places the civilian contractors actually built whole sections of the original road). The Kiskatinaw Bridge was built between November 1942 and the summer of 1943 by the Dow Construction Company of Toronto. It was one of many timber bridges built along the highway at that time, and like the others, weight limits eventually proved too light for modern traffic.

Here, however, a rerouting of the Alaska Highway in 1978 saved the bridge from demolition and replacement. Today it is used primarily by traffic bound for nearby Kiskatinaw Provincial Park. It is the only timber bridge still being used that was built on the original route of the Alaska Highway.

Alexander Mackenzie First to Cross the Continent
30.5 miles (49 km) north of Dawson Creek

In 1793, more than a decade before Lewis and Clark crossed the American West, North-West Company explorer Alexander

Mackenzie led the first expedition to cross the North American continent north of the Mexican border. After Mackenzie's journey, as the fur companies began operating west of the mountains, the Peace River became for a short time a link in Canada's first transcontinental transportation network connecting Montreal with the Pacific.

Mackenzie also was the first explorer to tell the world of the vast Yukon River, which lay farther north. In 1789, while still looking for a river that would lead across the Rocky Mountains to the Pacific, he followed his namesake river to its mouth on the Arctic Ocean. On the Mackenzie, which he called the River of Disappointment because it failed to lead to the Pacific, he learned from Indians of a river they called *Youcon,* or "big river," flowing northwest on the opposite side of the northern mountains.

No one paid much attention to the story of this river when Mackenzie published news of it in his journal. Later, though, after his report was translated into Russian, officials in the Russian-American Fur Company became extremely interested. They renewed their exploration of the Alaska coastline, following several rivers into the interior and eventually made the first European discovery of today's Yukon.

Peace River Destroys Longest Bridge on Alaska Highway
Peace River Bridge, 34.4 miles (55.5 km) north of Dawson Creek

---

In 1942, when a military ferry couldn't keep up with the huge amount of supplies and materiel moving north during the war, bridging the Peace River became the first major challenge to confront the builders of the Alaska Highway. After three failed attempts a wooden trestle bridge was finally completed in October 1942, but it washed away the following month. In December the same company that built the Brooklyn Bridge in New York was contracted to build a steel suspension bridge over the Peace.

The new structure became the longest bridge on the Alaska Highway. It was completed in 1943 but was still vulnerable to the ravages of the river. In 1957 the huge steel bridge collapsed under the force of the mighty Peace River just as the original wooden bridge had fallen 15 years earlier. Construction of today's bridge, somewhat shorter than the original, began almost immediately. It opened to traffic in 1960.

The Taylor Flats Dispute
Historic Milepost 35, 35 miles (56 km) north of Dawson Creek

Taylor Flats was given its name by Herbert Taylor, a Hudson's Bay Company trader who homesteaded on the north side of the river next to the ferry landing. A neighboring homesteader, Robert Barker, thought Barker Flats would be a more appropriate name. The two neighbors posted signs, each naming the place after himself. The government finally settled the matter when it called the first post office here Taylor.

Six Thousand Come to Camp Alcan
Historic Milepost 47, Fort St. John

In 1942 Fort St. John was near the end of an existing road from Dawson Creek, and it became a supply point for construction of the new road to Alaska. Before work on the Alaska Highway began, the town boasted 200 people. Almost overnight the arrival of soldiers at the new Camp Alcan sent Fort St. John's population soaring to 6,200.

Army construction crew erecting a pile driver on the Alaska Highway near Edith Creek in 1942.

Fort St. John was also the terminus of a trail that already existed from Fort Nelson, 300 miles (483 km) to the north. The old trail, though, was a grueling route that took a pack train of horses three weeks to complete. Although this trail was still regularly used in 1942—and had even recently been used by the Canadian military as a supply route for the construction of a Northwest Staging Route airstrip at Fort Nelson—surveyors staked out a new route from Fort St. John to Fort Nelson that left only small sections of today's road following the original trail.

View of one of the rows of tents at the U.S. Army's Camp White-horse on the Alaska Highway in 1942.

American soldiers—the 35th Engineers—did, however, push north to Fort Nelson on the old trail ahead of highway construction. While crews worked north from Fort St. John, the 35th Engineers went to Fort Nelson to work north from there. The building of the Alaska Highway throughout 1942 was always a many-pronged attack on the wilderness with soldier–construction workers starting from several points along today's highway. If the pioneer road had been built as a single slash, cutting north from Dawson Creek, construction would have taken much longer than eight months.

Soldiers of the U.S. Army's 18th Engineers stand around a truck stuck in the sand during construction of Alaska Highway in 1942.

In addition to the 35th pushing north from Fort Nelson, the 341st and 95th General Service regiments were working from Dawson Creek and Fort St. John. In the Yukon, troops arrived over the White Pass & Yukon Route railway from Skagway. The 18th Engineers worked north from Whitehorse, while the 93rd General Service Regiment headed south. From Carcross the 340th General Service Regiment traveled east to Teslin, where it began working toward Watson Lake. In Alaska the 97th Engineers worked southeast from the Richardson Highway after landing at Valdez, Alaska, on ships from the south.

Bulldozers prepare road bed on the Alaska Highway in 1942.

Each regiment contained approximately 1,000 enlisted men and 40 officers. They were supplied with about 20 D-8 tractors and bulldozers, 24 D-4 and R-4 tractors and bulldozers, two power shovels, 75 dump trucks, 12 pickups, 6 tractor-drawn graders, 6 twelve-yard (11-M) carryalls, 2 pile drivers, a portable sawmill and a truck crane.

One man wears mosquito netting as the U.S. Army 18th Engineers build the Cracker Creek Bridge on the Alaska Highway in June 1942.

Initially, the entire project was under the command of Colonel William M. Hoge. It soon became apparent that logistics required the command be separated into northern and southern sectors. Colonel James "Patsy" O'Connor took over responsibilities for the southern part of the highway between Dawson Creek and Watson Lake. Hoge, based in Whitehorse, took command of the larger northern sector between Watson Lake and Fairbanks.

First Settler in Fort St. John Murders Mountie
Fort St. John, 47 miles (76 km) north of Dawson Creek

In 1806 the North West Company established the original fur post at Fort St. John about 10 miles (16 km) from the present townsite. An earlier trading post, upriver from today's town, dates from 1794, which makes Fort St. John the oldest European community in British Columbia.

Fort St. John's first settler in the years after the establishment of North West Company and, later, Hudson's Bay Company fur posts was a black man named Daniel Williams. An escaped slave from Virginia, Williams came west in 1857 with the Palliser Expedition, which was investigating the suitability of western Canada for settlement. After he left the expedition, Williams turned to prospecting and trapping. He arrived in the Fort St. John area in 1869 and built a cabin on the north side of the Peace River directly opposite the Hudson's Bay Company post.

Williams staked a mining claim, planted a vegetable garden and settled in to stay. He also planted the first wheat crop ever grown in the Peace River country. During the long winters, he spent his time trapping in the surrounding wilderness.

In the winter of 1872–73, while Williams was away on his trapline, the Hudson's Bay Company decided to move its post to the north side of the river. By the time Williams returned, a new Hudson's Bay trading post was nearing completion right next to his cabin on land Williams figured belonged to him. Angered, he tacked a note to the fur post door warning the trader to move. I will not be "trodded upon by any but Her Majesty's Government," the note declared. Unfortunately, for Williams, the Hudson's Bay Company held more sway with the government than he did.

But Williams raged against the company transgressors for years. Then in 1879 he was finally arrested for attempted murder. According to a Hudson's Bay Company trader, Williams had shot at him and missed. A Mountie took Williams to Fort Saskatchewan for trial, but instead of choosing an Edmonton lawyer for his defense, Williams chose a colorful Peace River character named Banjo Mike.

McKinley, the Hudson's Bay trader, claimed that Williams had called, "I'll fix you," and then fired a shot that whizzed close to his ear. Banjo Mike told the jury that "I'll fix you" could have meant almost anything. He also pointed out that nobody could possibly tell, upon hearing a bullet, whether it was close to his ear, or 5 feet, 10 feet, or even 10 yards away. He stated further that Dan Williams was an expert marksman who could take the eye out of a jackrabbit at 100 yards. "If Dan Williams had the slightest intention of harming Mr. McKinley," Banjo Mike told the jury, "Mr. McKinley would not be here today to amuse you with his little story."

The jury found Williams innocent of the charge. That should have been the end of things, but Dan Williams was still angry at the Hudson's Bay Company. And he was also angry at the Mountie who had taken him in. The following year, he shot and killed the Mountie, then escaped to the wilderness where local Indians helped him hide for several months. Eventually, Williams was captured. This time he was hung for murder.

Route to Klondike Gold through Fort St. John
Fort St. John

In 1897, when the outside world learned of huge gold strikes near the Yukon River on tributaries of the Klondike, the largest, most exciting and zanniest gold rush in North American history began. One San Francisco newspaper reported that a "ton of gold" was aboard the first ship returning from Alaska that year. Actually, there were three tons, and soon thousands of people throughout the world were planning treks to the Yukon to get some of the yellow metal for themselves.

Most of the new gold seekers went up the British Columbia and Alaska coast, along the Inside Passage and over the White or Chilkoot Pass. For those with enough money, it was possible for a while in summer to take a steamer all the way to the new boomtown of Dawson City. A few stampeders struggled up the old telegraph trail through British Columbia. And several thousand misguided souls decided to start for the Yukon from the closest railway point. In those days that meant Edmonton, Alberta. From Edmonton these unfortunate gold rushers attempted to follow northern rivers and fur trails all the way to Dawson City.

Although the Edmonton Board of Trade was all for any route that would take thousands of gold seekers through their town, trails out of Edmonton were undoubtedly the worst of all the accepted routes to the Klondike. It's true that fur traders had followed these trails out of Edmonton on their way north for years, but new gold prospectors from Toronto, New York or Chicago were not veterans of the northern wilderness. The lucky ones, in fact, would be the stampeders who turned back early, and the earlier they turned back the luckier they were. Few who started from Edmonton even got as far as Fort St. John, where one of the more prominent routes left the Peace River and paralleled the route of today's Alaska Highway for much of the journey north.

That the gold seekers of the Klondike rush were novices in the wilderness is aptly demonstrated by the ways many of them attempted to travel. A fellow called Texas Smith, for instance, left Edmonton in a contraption that was, essentially, three huge wooden barrels fixed on shafts, tricycle-fashion, pulled by a horse. Smith presumed the barrels would roll over the muskeg and swamps all the way to Dawson City. Inside the barrels, he carried his prospecting supplies. Unfortunately, the hoops came off the barrels 7 miles (11 km) out of Edmonton, and Texas Smith followed a trail of beans and flour all the way back to the North Saskatchewan River.

Another group of gold seekers figured they could sail to the Yukon on a bed of northern ice. They built a huge ice boat complete with sails. Unfortunately, even if there had been clear sailing all the way to Dawson, which there wasn't, the weight of the boat was too much for any wind short of a hurricane to budge.

Perhaps the greatest boondoggle was the great steam sled constructed by a group from Chicago. A boiler and marine engine powered the sled, and spikelike teeth studded the engine wheels to provide traction. These wheels, it was reasoned, would be able to pull a train of four railroad cars riding on runners. On the day of its departure, the sled's engine started and the studded wheels began to spin, but the steam sled failed to move north. Instead, the wheels dug the whole works into the ground.

There were several routes to the Klondike out of Edmonton, but a majority of the Edmonton stampeders came through the Fort St. John area. Old fur trails between the Saskatchewan and Peace rivers near today's Alaska Highway had been in use for most of the previous century, so at least on paper, the overland route through Fort St. John seemed an attractive one.

Of the 1,500 to 2,000 stampeders who headed for the Yukon on one or the other of the overland routes from Edmonton, however, perhaps only a dozen made it to Dawson City in the first year. Only about 100 made it the next year. One couple conceived and bore a baby girl before they reached Dawson. Several people committed suicide. A few others settled down at points along the way and became trappers. Most gave up somewhere along the trail and went back to Edmonton.

Even the North-West Mounted Police had trouble on the overland route from Edmonton. Inspector J.D. Moodie and four constables were ordered to mark an overland trail through Fort St. John to the Yukon in September 1897. Moodie's party spent a year and a month completing the task. The return trip to his post in Maple Creek, Saskatchewan, via Skagway, took only 18 days.

Charlie Lake First Mile Zero
Historic Milepost 52, 4 miles (6 km) north of Fort St. John

Because roads existed as far north as Charlie Lake in 1942, for a time in the early days of the construction of the Alaska Highway, the army called this point Mile Zero. Other spots along the highway, built by different construction crews, were also known as Mile Zero. Eventually, Dawson Creek was confirmed as the official one. The spot where the Alcan joined the Richardson Highway in Alaska, at today's Delta Junction, is now designated the end of the Alaska Highway, 1,420 miles (2285 km) north of Dawson Creek.

But controversy still surrounds both claims. The highway was, after all, constructed to make a road connection with Fairbanks. All early documents specify that the Alaska Highway was to reach that city. A milepost marking the end of the highway was even placed near the river in downtown Fairbanks. Yet, because there was already a road between Fairbanks and Delta Junction—or Buffalo Crossing as the place was known at the time—it is logical to place the end of the new Alaska Highway there. On the other hand, there was also an existing road between Dawson Creek and Charlie Lake in 1942, so the same logic should make Charlie Lake the official Mile Zero.

Beatton River Air Base Built
Historic Milepost 73, 25.8 miles (42 km) north of Fort St. John

In addition to the Alaska Highway, the American and Canadian military built a series of flight strips between southern Canada and Alaska to beef up the Northwest Staging Route. The Beatton River Strip was the first of these air bases.

Beatton River was originally called the Epinette by early fur traders. Later, it was called the North Pine. Finally, in the early 1900s it was named for Frank Beatton, an early Hudson's Bay Company trader at Fort St. John.

Blueberry Control Gate at Wonowon
Historic Milepost 101, Wonowon, 54 miles (87 km) north of Fort St. John

During World War II Wonowon was the site of a control gate for the Alaska Highway. During the war, anyone driving the road, including Canadian citizens, had to receive permission from the American army before proceeding. A 24-hour checkpoint known as the Blueberry Control Gate was built here. Before the construction of the highway, the settlement of Wonowon (at Mile 101) was named Blueberry, after the Blueberry River.

Sikanni Hill Once Called Suicide Hill
Historic Milepost 148, 43.7 miles (70 km) north of Wonowon

In the early years of the highway the grade on Sikanni Hill was so steep that a sign posted at the top proclaimed, "Be prepared to meet thy God." Everyone called the place Suicide Hill. Accidents were common. Eventually, however, the highway was relocated to a point slightly west, where the grade could be improved, and the name Suicide Hill was abandoned to history. Today, after highway improvements, the place is known as Sikanni Hill.

Fort Nelson Wiped Out in Indian Attack
Historic Milepost 300, 236 miles (380 km) north of Fort St. John

The first European settlement in the Fort Nelson area came when the North West Company built a fur post on the banks of the Fort Nelson River in 1805. Rather typically, fur posts here changed their location several times during the intervening years. Perhaps for 50 of those years there was no post on the river at all.

In 1813 Indians attacked and burned Fort Nelson, killing the trader and seven family members. Over 50 years later, in 1865, the Hudson's Bay Company reestablished a fur post here, mostly in an attempt to thwart free-traders in this area.

Gradually, a permanent settlement grew up around the fur post at Fort Nelson, but the community remained an isolated outpost until the outbreak of World War II. Then the Canadian government built an airstrip nearby as part of the Northwest Staging Route. Early in 1942 two thousand soldiers in the American army arrived over the old freight trail leading north from Fort St. John. They established a base camp here for the construction of the Fort Nelson to Whitehorse leg of the Alaska Highway. Since Fort Nelson was the starting point for the work going north, it, too, became Mile Zero—one of several such points on the highway during the construction period.

$32,000 in Furs Stolen from Hudson's Bay Company Store
Fort Nelson

In the summer of 1936 two masked men robbed the Hudson's Bay trading post at Fort Nelson of 29 bales of furs that had just been prepared for shipment south. The furs were valued at $32,000, or $384,00 in today's dollars. Constable J.S. Clark and Game Warden Baptiste Villeneuve of the Fort Nelson Police and Game Department spent nearly 14 months trying to solve the case. Early on, they thought they knew who committed the crime—two local trappers named Henry Courvoisier and Bert Sheffield—but they couldn't prove anything without the stolen furs.

Then early in August 1937, an Indian by the name of Netsena heard a noise as he paddled down the Fort Nelson River. Thinking he had heard a bear, he stopped to investigate. Instead of a bear, however, Netsena found the bales of furs, many of them opened and spread out in the sun. The noise he heard was Sheffield and Courvoisier. They had returned to their cache of looted furs and were sorting through them when Netsena had stopped to investigate. Hiding in the trees above, they watched as he discovered the furs.

Knowing the story of the stolen furs, Netsena relayed word back to Fort Nelson that he had found them. Soon, officers Clark and Villeneuve arrived, but all the while, Sheffield and Courvoisier watched from the trees. The two thieves were worried because Sheffield had written his name on one of the tarps that covered the furs. This, of course, would link them to the stolen pelts.

That night, even though the stolen furs and incriminating tarp had been put under armed guard, Sheffield and Courvoisier were able to sneak in and set them on fire. Then the two men escaped into the wilderness, working their way south, often swimming lakes and rivers to cover their trail. Eventually, the pair of desperadoes made their way to Fort St. John. Here, they traded their horses for a car, then drove to Edmonton where they took a bus to Sweetgrass, Montana. But at the border the pair aroused the suspicions of an American customs official, who had them arrested and returned to British Columbia. After they were tried and convicted, the Hudson's Bay Company gave Netsena a $500 reward.

Alaska Highway Sells Postcards and Dust
Fort Nelson

North of Fort Nelson the first good views of the Rocky Mountains begin to appear from the highway. As the road passes from the foothills to mountains it enters the rugged terrain often depicted on photographs and postcards. Sometimes pushed against the nearly perpendicular sides of the mountains themselves, the highway hugs the shores of sparkling green lakes and the banks of mountains streams. Always, the spruce forests crowd the road until, from the top of some rise or pass, a panoramic vista suddenly pops into view like the next frame in the slide show.

This spectacular setting and the legends of it promoted throughout North America inspired tourists to take to the road even before the end of World War II. Once the war ended, the trickle of tourists turned into a flood. In 1945, the Chicago Motor League conducted a poll and reported that three million Americans were planning major post-war car trips, and 20 percent of these said they were going to drive the Alaska Highway. After the war ended, new businesses were born up and down the new road to provide services to northern tourists.

In Fort Nelson, Earl Bartlett, an electrician who had come to the community in 1943, began taking photographs of scenic spots along the highway. He turned these photographs into picture postcards, which he sold at highway stops between Dawson Creek and the Alaska border. By the time of his death, Bartlett had sold well over one million postcards.

Perhaps the strangest successful business to take root on the highway was spawned by a group of Whitehorse entrepreneurs. In 1964 these enterprising souls started canning Alaska Highway dust, which tourists snapped up every summer, particularly in dry dusty years. A guarantee on the label of each can promised that if, after eating the dust, the buyer was unsatisfied in any way, another can would be provided at cost.

One of the first new businesses along the Alaska Highway opened its doors to commerce 50 miles (81 km) south of Fort Nelson, near the Prophet River. In 1942 army engineers cut the new highway right past an old log cabin belonging to a pair of longtime trappers in the area. The aging men, as with most trappers in the North , had spent most of their lives without much human companionship.

With the coming of the highway, everything changed. Suddenly, all sorts of people were traveling by their door all the time. The two trappers were so happy to see all the new people that they hung up a sign and opened a restaurant to lure in guests. The menu was sparse. All the men served was pancakes and coffee, but they were open 24 hours a day 7 days a week. Only a small table sat in the middle of the cabin, but as many as eight people could crowd in to eat at the same time. Plain, blueberry and raspberry pancakes were served along with coffee. Refills were free and so was the constant conversation of the two old trappers.

Bush Pilots Scout Highway Route through Mountains
Historic Milepost 443, 140 miles (225 km) north of Fort Nelson

The bridge here crosses Peterson Creek, a stream named after a local trapper who helped surveyors find a route for the Alaska Highway through this area in 1942. The portion of highway to be built between Fort Nelson and Teslin in the Yukon comprised the longest stretch of road without major established trails that surveyors had to deal with before construction could begin.

In addition to guides on the ground, bush pilots were hired to look for possible routes across the mountains. Colonel William Hoge, commanding officer in charge of highway construction in 1942, flew hundreds of miles with Canadian pilot Les Cook, whom Hoge credited with shortening the highway more than 100 miles (161 km). Hoge and Cook discovered the Rancheria River route between Watson Lake and Teslin. Cook, however, barely lived to see the highway in use. In December 1942 he died in his plane after a fiery crash on the streets of Whitehorse.

Most of the guides hired during the construction of the Alaska Highway were native trappers. Southerners tended to think, and rightly so, that Yukon Indians knew pretty well everything about the lay of the country and how to get around in it. On the other hand, many areas along the highway weren't known well by anyone. A Tlingit trapper and guide from Teslin Lake later told how he and the other guides tried to keep far enough ahead of their American employers to have time to scout out a route through the unfamiliar areas. Sometimes, he reported, they would have to climb trees to see where they were.

Price of Muncho Lake Road Highest on Highway
Historic Milepost 456, Muncho Lake, 152.5 miles (245 km) north of Fort Nelson

The Alaska Highway builders encountered great difficulty as they cut the road along the east side of Muncho Lake's rocky shore. At an elevation of nearly 2,700 feet (823M), Muncho Lake is 7 miles (11 km) long and tucked into the side of the Sentinel Range of the Rocky Mountains. The original surveyors chose this route instead of the longer and even more costly traditional route through the Grand Canyon of the Liard River.

Nevertheless, this section of road, snaking through the rocky bluffs along the east shore, proved to be the most expensive section of the highway to build. Horse-drawn stone boats were used to haul away excavated rock from the lake's shore. No one kept track of the machinery and equipment lost over the rocky ledges into the waters of the 300-foot- (91-M-) deep lake.

Muncho Lake was also the sight of a Signal Corps and Northwest Service Command maintenance camp during World War II. The Command was created in the early days of the war to oversee activity in the Canadian and American Northwest. This included responsibility for the construction of the Alaska Highway, the Edmonton to Fairbanks telephone link and the Canol Oil Pipeline.

Suspension Bridge on Alaska Highway Crosses First Highway to the Yukon
Liard River, 40 miles (64 km) north of Muncho Lake

The only suspension bridge left on the Alaska Highway crosses the lower Liard River here. The Liard was named by French Canadian voyageurs working for the Hudson's Bay Company for the poplar trees, or "liard," that grow so profusely along the river.

In 1840, Robert Campbell followed the Liard on his way to discovering the first fur trade route into the Yukon Valley. Campbell traveled the Liard into today's Yukon Territory, becoming the first white man to go there, and then crossed the divide north of today's Watson Lake to the Pelly River, which fed into the Yukon. This route was used for three years to supply Fort Selkirk at the mouth of the Pelly. Then, in 1851, Campbell began using a new route, supplying his fort from the Mackenzie River Delta via the Porcupine River and Fort Yukon. All during the 19th century, though, Hudson's Bay traders and canoe men considered the Liard the most dangerous of all the northern rivers. Some, in fact, after their terms of service with the company had ended and knowing how many of their fellows had drowned here, only re-enlisted after first demanding assurances that their duties would never include travel on the Liard River.

Alaska Highway Opens Liard River Hot Springs
Historic Milepost 496, .75 miles (1.2 km) north of Lower Liard Bridge

Legends of the hot springs on the Liard River had been told for years before the construction of the Alaska Highway. Tales reached the outside world of a northern tropical paradise where exotic animals roamed and a garden of junglelike greenery lasted all winter. Then in 1942 construction of the Alaska Highway brought workers close enough to the fabled waters for builders to cut a trail to the springs, making them accessible to outsiders for the first time.

After the war, the meager facilities built by the army fell into disrepair, but in the early 1950s local volunteers rebuilt the boardwalk trails and cleaned up the campsites. Almost immediately the hot springs became a favorite stopping place for the thousands of tourists who travel the highway every summer and a year-round diversion for local people along the same road.

Smith River Airport Built in 1942
Historic Milepost 514, 18 miles (30 km) north of Lower Liard River Bridge

The Smith River Airport and Road were built during World War II as part of the Northwest Staging Route. This network of airstrips served air traffic between the Soviet Union, Alaska, the Yukon and southern areas of North America. Ultimately, it had been the airstrips of the Northwest Staging Route that had determined the course of the Alaska Highway itself. Military strategists were never convinced of the necessity of the highway as a supply route to Alaska, but most of them saw clearly how the road could supply the airfields of the Northwest Staging Route, whose strategic importance to the war effort was never questioned. In fact, because of the presence of the highway, military planners decided to build additional air fields along the route, bolstering the military air supply line to Alaska and eastern Europe, and increasing its safety. The Smith River Airstrip became one of the first of these additional landing facilities made possible by the Alaska Highway.

Contact Made at Contact Creek
Historic Milepost 588, 91 miles (147 km) north of Lower Liard River Bridge

On September 24, 1942, soldiers of the 35th Regiment, who were building the highway north from Fort Nelson, met builders of the 340th Regiment working south from Whitehorse at this spot. Within a week the highway was open as far as Whitehorse. This left only the stretch of road through the western Yukon and eastern Alaska to be completed. Finally, on October 29, 1942, less than eight months after construction had begun, the Alaska Highway's pioneer road, which totaled a remarkable 1,619 miles (2,606 km) between Dawson Creek and Fairbanks, would be finished.

Hudson's Bay Company Opens Lower Post
Alaska Highway, Lower Post Junction, 30.5 miles (49 km) north of Contact Creek Bridge

A gravel road leading south at this point leads to Lower Post, a former Indian village and the site of an early Hudson's Bay Company trading post. Located at the junction of the Liard and Dease rivers, Lower Post was a stopping-off point for trappers and miners heading north on the Liard River in the 1880s. Over the years, the community went by a variety of names including Lower Post, Sylvester Post and Liard Post.

The first log trading post here was built by Rufus Sylvester in the 1870s. In 1942, the original route of the Alaska Highway went directly through the small settlement. The army ran a sawmill here, cutting timber for bridge building. Later, civilian contractors rerouted the highway to the north as the road was upgraded and improved.

Robert Campbell First to Enter the Yukon
Lucky Lake Picnic Area, Alaska Highway, 10 miles (16 km) north of Lower Post Junction

A two-mile (three-kilometer) trail from the Lucky Lake Recreational Area leads to the Liard River Canyon. The precipitous banks of the often raging Liard often stand dozens of feet above water, so that sometimes not even a foothold can be found anywhere below the cliff tops. On the opposite side of the river, a cairn here is dedicated to Robert Campbell, who is believed to have been the first European to enter the Yukon Territory.

Campbell followed the Liard River into the Yukon in 1840. Over the next few years he established trading posts for the Hudson's Bay Company, including Fort Selkirk, which he built on what he called the Pelly River, on the Yukon at the mouth of today's Pelly, 1848. Three years later, Campbell followed the course of his Pelly as far as Fort Youcon at the mouth of the Porcupine. This established for the first time that Campbell's Fort Selkirk and the Hudson's Bay Company's Fort Youcon were both on the same river.

Although the Liard was the route to the Yukon for Robert Campbell, the river proved to be one of the most dangerous of all the routes for Klondike stampeders 50 years later. In fact, many stampeders who chose to follow the Liard were still struggling up the river in 1899, two years after they had set out for the Klondike. Of the men and women who chose to follow the Liard, the fortunate ones gave up early and went home. Many of those who struggled on died along the trail. Only a few ever made it to Dawson City.

Frank Watson Quits Gold Rush at Watson Lake
Historic Milepost 635, Alaska Highway, Watson Lake, 55 miles (89 km) north of Contact Creek Bridge

---

Frank Watson left Edmonton on the overland route to the Klondike early in 1897. A year later he was still on the trail. Like so many others, Watson discovered that the all-Canadian route was perhaps the worst possible way to reach the gold fields. North-West Mounted Police Inspector Sam Steele went so far as to say that no sane person would attempt it.

Watson stuck to the trail for more than a year, but in the spring of 1898, still on the upper Liard River, he decided he was unlikely to find any better country than where he was. He stopped, built a cabin on the shore of what we now know as Watson Lake, married an Indian woman named Adela Stone and turned to hunting and trapping for a living.

The town of Watson Lake was born four years after Frank Watson's death, when an airfield was built nearby in the early days of World War II. The airport was part of the Northwest Staging Route, the series of northern airfields that provided fuel and service stops during the war for military aircraft bound for Alaska and the Soviet Union.

Construction of the Alaska Highway linked Watson's Lake with the outside world, and after its completion the town grew as a service center for highway travelers. It also became a supply center for mining and logging industries in the southern Yukon and northern British Columbia. The log runway terminal constructed when the Watson Lake Airport was first built has now been designated an historic building.

Sign Forest Grows at Watson Lake
Alaska Highway, Watson Lake, 55 miles (89 km) north of Contact Creek Bridge

In 1942 Carl Lindley of Danville, Illinois, was a homesick American soldier working with the 341st Engineers on the construction of the Alaska Highway. Assigned the task of refurbishing road signs, Lindley took time out to make a sign of his own. He painted the name of his hometown on a board, along with an arrow pointing south and the miles that had to be covered to get there. Then he tacked up his sign at a prominent place on the highway near Watson Lake.

Other soldiers had done the same kind of thing up and down the Alaska Highway from Dawson Creek to Fairbanks, but in Watson Lake the idea took hold. Before long, other soldiers began nailing up signs for their towns. Then other travelers on the highway began to do the same thing and the Watson Lake sign forest began to grow. Today thousands of signs from all over the world have been added to Lindley's. In 1990 Olen and Anita Walker of Bryan, Ohio, put up the 10,000th sign at the Watson Lake sign forest. Every year since then the forest has continued to grow until today visitors who spend the time looking are almost assured of finding familiar signs from their own region, no matter where in North America and, in some cases the world, they happen to come from.

Side Trip:
Robert Campbell Highway from Watson Lake

Robert Campbell First in the Yukon
Junction of Robert Campbell Highway and Alaska Highway,
Watson Lake

Opened in 1968 the Robert Campbell Highway stretches from Watson Lake for 373 miles (600 km) across the south-central Yukon to its junction with the Klondike Highway just north of the town of Carmacks. For much of that distance the highway parallels a route to the Yukon River used by early fur traders, beginning with the Hudson's Bay Company trader Robert Campbell.

Campbell was the first European to explore what is today the Yukon Territory. It was Campbell who named many of the rivers and lakes along today's Campbell Highway. Most of the names he chose were for his superiors in the Hudson's Bay Company. Simpson Lake, the large body of water 50 miles (80 km) north of Watson Lake on today's highway, for instance, he named after Hudson's Bay Governor George Simpson. The Pelly River, which the highway parallels beginning 12 miles (19 km) beyond Finlayson Lake, Campbell named for another company governor, John Henry Pelly. Pelly later wrote to Campbell suggesting that the river be called Campbell instead, but Campbell refused the honor. This turned out to be a decision he regretted later in his life—after the Hudson's Bay Company suddenly and unjustly fired him for sending furs out of the country without authorization during the Riel Rebellion of 1870.

Robert Campbell first came to the Yukon in 1840. With three companions—two Indian guides and another employee of the fur company—he traveled up the Liard River into today's Yukon Territory. From the mouth of the Liard, Campbell poled up the Frances River, then crossed the continental divide to the Pelly. The Russians had discovered the lower reaches of the Yukon River, where it flows into the Bering Sea at Norton Sound, six years earlier, but they had penetrated only a short distance up the river into the Alaska interior. When Campbell crossed the divide to the Pelly, he became the first European trader on the upper Yukon watershed.

In the spring of 1843 Campbell returned to the Pelly with eight other men and followed it to its junction with the Yukon, which he called the Lewes (naming the river after yet another Hudson's Bay Company official). Here, Campbell encountered Tutchone Indians who told him they had never before seen white men. The Indians knew about whites, however. In fact they regularly traded for Russian and American goods with Chilkat Indians from the Alaska coast. The Tutchone also told Campbell of another tribe of Indians farther downriver who, they said, killed and ate anyone they could catch. Campbell scoffed at the story, but his men refused to go farther.

The following year, when Hudson's Bay Governor George Simpson saw Campbell's report of his journey to the junction of the Pelly and Lewes rivers, the governor sent Campbell back to the Yukon. This time Campbell was instructed to open a trading post in the area. This he did, first on the banks of the Pelly in 1846, then on the Yukon River at the mouth of the Pelly in 1848.

Not long after Campbell began exploring the Yukon watershed from the south, another Hudson's Bay trader, John Bell, entered the country from the north. Bell first explored the lower Peel River in 1840, then returned to open Fort McPherson at the edge of the Mackenzie and Peel River Delta, in today's Northwest Territories. In 1842, Bell traveled from the Peel up the Rat River, and after a rugged portage over the Richardson Mountains, he reached the Porcupine River in today's Yukon Territory. Bell decided the overland route was too difficult to supply a trading post on the west side of the mountains, so he returned to Fort McPherson and forwarded his recommendations to the Hudson's Bay Company.

Governor Simpson wanted to push his trading empire farther west, so despite Bell's report of the difficulties of the supply route, he ordered Bell to explore the Porcupine to its mouth with the idea of eventually establishing a fur post deep in the heart of Russian North America. In 1844 Bell followed the river until it joined a larger river that he said the Kutchin Indians called "Youcon." Three years later Alexander Murray, a 27-year-old fur trader who had previously worked for the American Fur Company, was sent to open a post here called Fort Youcon, or Yukon.

The English company knew that their post lay deep in Russian territory, but they chose to ignore the ill-defined border, assuming correctly that the Russians hadn't penetrated the interior far enough to create a problem. But Murray built a stockade anyway to protect against a possible Russian attack. He knew the Russians already had posts on the lower reaches of a large river he assumed correctly was the Yukon. The Russians could easily follow the river east if they wanted to enforce their claim to the territory. But no one ever tried to drive Murray away. In fact it would be 25 years before the location of Fort Yukon would be challenged, and then it would be Alaska's new American owners who would complain.

Meanwhile, upstream on the Yukon, Robert Campbell at Fort Selkirk suspected, but had no first-hand proof, that his post and Fort Yukon were on the same river. At Fort Selkirk, Campbell found the Indians friendly and strictly honest, but he had difficulty trading because the coastal Chilkat Indians traded better and cheaper Russian and American goods in the area. Hudson's Bay Company goods couldn't compete.

In 1851 Campbell finally proved that his post at Fort Selkirk and Murray's at Fort Yukon were on the same waterway. Governor Simpson had given Campbell permission earlier in the year to explore downstream on the river he called the Pelly. That summer, after only a few days of travel, Campbell drifted along the Yukon to the northern fur post at the mouth of the Porcupine. This trip confirmed what he had long suspected: His Pelly and Murray's Yukon, which was supplied from Fort MacPherson via the Porcupine, were the same river.

As soon as Campbell discovered the river connection with Fort Yukon, he traveled up the Porcupine to Fort McPherson, obtained trade articles and brought them back to Fort Selkirk. This gave him additional goods, which cost less than anything he could bring in over the shorter but more difficult southern route to the Yukon. For the first time he was able to compete effectively with the Chilkat.

The following summer, more of the cheaper trade goods arrived from Fort MacPherson, but Campbell hadn't reckoned on the wrath of the Chilkat. They quietly seethed over the actions of their new competitor until they attacked without warning and pillaged Fort Selkirk, forcing Campbell to run for his life. They would have killed him if the nearby Northern Tutchone Chief Hanan had not taken him in. Hanan supplied Campbell with food and shelter until it was safe to leave the area. Following Indian custom, Campbell gave the chief his name in gratitude. To this day Hanan's descendants use the Campbell family name.

After his rescue by Hanan, Campbell set out on snowshoes, traveling through the autumn and winter of 1852 until he arrived in Minnesota. From there he took a train to Montreal. Once back in Quebec, Campbell tried to persuade officials of the Hudson's Bay Company to mount a raid against the Chilkat and reestablish his Yukon River trading post. The Hudson's Bay Company declined to take up the challenge.

Campbell continued to work for the company as an administrator until his dismissal in 1871. He spent the last years of his life as a cattle rancher in Manitoba and never returned to the Yukon. It took another 40 years before a trading post was reestablished at Fort Selkirk. By then, however, men were primarily in the Yukon looking for gold, not furs. The new trader at Fort Selkirk was an Irish-American trader and prospector named Arthur Harper. (More about Robert Campbell and Arthur Harper can be found in Part I, the Klondike Highway.)

Nahani Range Road Built to Supply Miners
Robert Campbell Highway, Miner's Junction, 68.5 miles (110 km) north of Watson Lake

---

The Robert Campbell Highway and Nahani Range Road meet at this point. The Nahani Road was built in the 1960s, linking the Yukon with a Tungsten mine at the company town of Cantung in the Northwest Territories 125 miles (201 km) northeast of here. The mine closed in 1986 and the town's 500 residents moved out. Today the road is maintained for only the first 80 miles (129 km).

Frances Lake First Fur Post in Yukon
Frances Lake Historic Site, Robert Campbell Highway, 109 miles (175 km) north of Watson Lake

---

A Yukon government campground is located on the site of Fort Frances, the first fur post in the Yukon. Robert Campbell built the fort in 1842 and named it after Frances Simpson, wife of Hudson's Bay Governor George Simpson. The post here was abandoned in 1851 after Campbell discovered his post at Fort Selkirk could be supplied more easily from Fort MacPherson via Fort Yukon. The following year, after the Chilkat drove Campbell from Fort Selkirk, the Hudson's Bay Company abandoned the area for another 40 years.

Finlayson Lake Named in 1840
Finlayson Lake Historic Site, Robert Campbell Highway, 149 miles (240 km) north of Watson Lake

---

In 1840 Robert Campbell named Finlayson Lake after Duncan Finlayson, one of the Hudson's Bay Company's board of directors. Finlayson was a prominent supporter of Campbell in his bid to explore the region we know today as the Yukon Territory. The lake is 10 miles (16 km) long and sits on the upper reaches of the continental divide. Water from the lake drains into the Liard River on its way to the Mackenzie River and eventually the Arctic Ocean. Water just north of the lake drains into the Yukon and eventually the Pacific.

Canol Road Supplies Oil During World War II
Robert Campbell Highway, 159 miles (256 km) north of Miner's Junction

---

The Canol Road was constructed during World War II as part of the Canadian Oil Project. It was built to service the pipeline bringing oil 600 miles (966 km) from wells in the Northwest Territories to a refinery in Whitehorse. The initial reason for building the pipeline was to provide an alternate source of fuel for military aircraft along the Northwest Staging Route as well as vehicles along the newly constructed Alaska Highway. Gasoline for Alaska was normally brought up the Inside Passage on tankers from California, but some members of the American army worried that the Japanese navy could disrupt shipping and make supplies from California unreliable.

Almost from the beginning, however, the Canol pipeline proved to be a costly and problem-ridden undertaking. The project rivaled the Alaska Highway in engineering difficulties and in the end proved to be more costly. None of the major river valley routes from Norman Wells appeared practical, so engineers took the pipeline along a traditional native trail through the high country of the Mackenzie Mountains.

The pipeline between Norman Wells and the refinery built at Whitehorse was finally completed in February 1944. The cost was estimated at $3 million. Even then, however, the Canol project didn't supply much Alaskan oil. Needs were estimated at 13 tanker loads per month while the Whitehorse refinery supplied less than one. The cost, at about $10.45 per barrel, was more than twice that of tanker oil, which flowed north unimpeded by the Japanese throughout the war. By April 1945 the army declared the Canol Pipeline "surplus to its needs." The refinery in White-horse was sold to Imperial Oil for $1 million—$23 million less than it cost. Later, it was dismantled and shipped to Alberta.

The pipeline, along with construction and maintenance equipment left along the Canol Road, was sold to a salvaging company, which took out anything that appeared profitable and left everything else behind. Truck engines were generally removed, for instance, but truck bodies were left in dumps along the road. Today, several World War II vehicle and equipment dumps can still be found along the old road. Travel beyond the Northwest Territories border at Macmillan Pass is unsafe for vehicles.

Ross River Trading Post Runs 42 Years
7 miles (11 km) east of Robert Campbell Highway on Canol Road

The town of Ross River grew up around a trading post established at the junction of the Ross and Pelly rivers in 1903. The river had been named 60 years before by Robert Campbell for Hudson's Bay Company factor Donald Ross. For a time the trading post at Ross River went by the name Nahanni House because a number of Indians from the Nahanni area of the Northwest Territories came there to trade and trap. The original Ross River post was later taken over by the Whitehorse firm of Taylor and Drury. It continued its operations under various owners until 1945.

Yukon's Largest Mine at Faro
33 miles (53 km) north of Ross River Junction and 5.5 miles north of Robert Campbell Highway

The town of Faro, named after the popular gambling game, was built in 1969 when the open-pit Anvil Mine—which produced lead, zinc and silver—opened nearby. The mine largely owed its existence to a prospector named Al Kulan, who came north in 1947 and, though prospecting throughout the Yukon, concentrated on the Ross River area.

Using Indian guides, Kulan made several promising finds in the area, but nothing came of his discoveries for several years. Then in the 1960s Kulan joined forces with a University of California geologist named Aaro Aho to form Dynasty Explorations. Dynasty sent field crews into the Yukon to explore Kulan's most promising properties and eventually joined forces with the California-based Cypress Mines. By 1965 the company had more than a hundred people exploring Kulan's Yukon sites. By 1966, word of Kulan's discoveries leaked out and over 17,000 additional claims were staked in the area. Three years later Cypress Anvil, with new partners from around the world, opened what became the Yukon's largest mine at Faro.

By the early 1970s the Cypress Anvil Mine had become the backbone of the Yukon economy, but like most mining properties, it was built on a shaky foundation. In 1981 the mine closed, the victim of corporate financial problems and federal government interference. By that time, the mine was owned by Dome Petroleum, which saw its Yukon operation as only a minor component of its overall business. Within four years, the community of Faro had all but closed down, with only 300 of its former 2,000 residents still living there. The White Pass & Yukon Route railway was also devastated by the mine's closure and the old gold rush rail line shut down its operations, too. Then, as lead and zinc prices improved, the mine was reopened under new owners in the 1980s, only to be shut down again in 1996. Mining is a volatile business, however, always dependent upon the price of metal and other variables such as the international exchange rate of the Canadian dollar. Most analysts agree, however, that it is only a matter of time before the mine at Faro reopens to become one of the Yukon's largest employers once more.

Paddle Wheeler *Columbian* Explodes
Eagle's Nest Bluff, Robert Campbell Highway, 91 miles (147 km) west of Faro Junction

One of the worst steamboat accidents on the Yukon River occurred when the paddle-wheeler *Columbian* blew up and burned after crew members shooting ducks from the ship's deck accidentally fired a rifle into three tons of black powder stacked on board. The powder was part of a cargo of fruits, vegetables, hog carcasses and live cattle bound for Dawson City.

Captain J.O. Williams was at the wheel at the time of the accident, and he steered the *Columbian* hard toward the river-bank the moment he heard the explosion. This probably saved several lives, although the river steamer *Victorian* arrived on the scene soon afterward. Seven people were killed. The *Victorian* took the dead and wounded back to Whitehorse.

Carmack Builds Trading Post at Carmacks
Carmacks, Klondike Highway, 2 miles (3 km) south of junction with the Robert Campbell Highway

The Robert Campbell Highway ends two miles (three kilometers) north of the town of Carmacks, which is named for George Washington Carmack, who, with his two friends Tagish Charlie and Skookum Jim, discovered gold on a tributary of the Klondike River on August 17, 1896.

Three years before his great gold discovery, Carmack had started a trading post near what became the present village of Carmacks. After he discovered a coal deposit on nearby Tantalus Butte, Carmack built a cabin here and traded furs with local Indians, planning to develop a mine. Nothing ever came of Carmack's coal mine, but the town, thanks largely to his gold discovery in the Klondike, became an important stopping point on the Yukon River. Today it is the largest community on the Klondike Highway between Dawson City and Whitehorse.

Returning to the Alaska Highway at Watson Lake

Upper Liard Bridge Crosses Fur Trade River
Alaska Highway, 6 miles (10 km) west of Watson Lake

The Alaska Highway crosses the Liard River for the second time on the Upper Liard Bridge. The Liard River was an important fur trade route during the 19th century, providing access to the western side of the mountains into northern British Columbia and the Yukon Territory. The Liard is a treacherous river, however, and at least 14 Hudson's Bay Company employees were drowned freighting goods on its waters. Once Robert Campbell found that Fort Selkirk, his post on the Yukon River, could be supplied from the north, he used that route instead of the costlier and more dangerous one up the Liard.

Gold Discovered in Cassiar Region
Historic Milepost 649, Alaska Highway junction with Highway 37, 14 miles (23 km) west of Watson Lake

Highway 37, which joins the Alaska Highway here, can be used as an alternate road into the Yukon instead of the southern sections of the Alaska Highway. A minor gold rush occurred in this region immediately south of today's Alaska Highway beginning in 1875. At this time more than 20 years before the Klondike gold discovery that opened the Yukon and much of Alaska to the outside world, prospectors had already begun to notice a pattern of gold discoveries along the spine of the Rocky Mountains. Over the years, they followed the mountains north from Colorado to Montana and Idaho, and from the Frazer River and Cariboo regions of British Columbia into the Cassiar District. Finally, beginning in 1896 this pattern of gold discovery ended with the greatest gold rush of them all, the Klondike Stampede of 1897–98.

Spanish Name Given to River
Bridge over Lower Rancheria River, Alaska Highway, 50 miles (81 km) west of Watson Lake

Rancheria River was given its name by early Yukon prospectors who also had mined in California. *Rancheria* was a Spanish name for a farm settlement, but miners in California often used it to denote Indian villages. In the Yukon they applied the same word to a native village along this river. Eventually, the term was given to the river, too.

Lodges Built on Alaska Highway
Alaska Highway, 73 miles (118 km) west of Watson Lake

An Alaska Highway Anniversary Interpretive Panel here describes the importance and history of early lodges along the Alaska Highway. After the war, communities of sorts developed along the highway between the large centers such as Fort St. John, Fort Nelson, Watson Lake and Whitehorse. The new residents were the proprietors and workers in the scattered highway lodges and way stations that sprouted up and down the highway as the first northern visitors came north on the highway in the 1940s. Usually, at least 50 miles (80 km) apart, these outposts were little more than dots in the wilderness, no more than a blink to passing motorists, but collectively they provided the services that made travel on the Alaska Highway possible.

Pine Lake Airstrip Built Near Highway
Historic Milepost 722, Alaska Highway, 88 miles (142 km) from Watson Lake

An historical marker here commemorates the construction of the Pine Lake Airstrip, one of a series of airstrips built to augment the major air bases on the Northwest Staging Route. In fact, as things turned out, it was the construction of the airstrips on the Northwest Staging Route that became the most important military benefit derived from building the Alaska Highway into the far Northwest.

Longest Bridge on Alaska Highway at Teslin
Historic Milepost 804, Alaska Highway, 162 miles (261 km) west of Watson Lake

The bridge over Nisultin Bay, where the Nisutlin River empties into Teslin Lake, is the longest bridge on the entire route of the Alaska Highway. Although the original Peace River suspension bridge was 200 feet (61M) longer than the Nisutlin Bay Bridge's 1,917 feet (584M), that bridge collapsed in 1957. Today's bridge over the Peace River is slightly shorter than the Nisutlin.

George Johnston Brings First Automobile to Teslin Lake
West side of Nisutlin Bay Bridge, Teslin

Hunter, trapper, merchant, photographer and Tlingit band member George Johnston brought the first automobile to Teslin Lake in 1928. This was before the community could boast of a road of any sort, let alone a highway leading south to the outside world. After he bought his 1928 Chevrolet, Johnston built three miles (five km) of road along Teslin Lake and sold rides in his car for a small fee. The vehicle became known as the Teslin Taxi. In the winter, Johnston added chains to the tires and drove on the lake ice.

Teslin Residents Doubt Story of Highway
West Side of Nisutlin Bay Bridge, Teslin

In the early spring of 1942, long before the snow began to melt, a Tlingit Indian arrived in Teslin Lake telling residents of hundreds of American soldiers with bulldozers and trucks tearing a path through the wilderness between Carcross and their lake. The people in Teslin liked this messenger from outside. They had always believed him to be an honest man, but the news he brought was too farfetched. No one would believe him no matter how much he protested that he was telling the truth. Then a few days later, the first American bulldozers crashed through the trees along the lake and the messenger was proved truthful after all.

The American army had cut cross-country from the railroad at Carcross to get a jump on construction that had already started east from Whitehorse. From Teslin, the army continued building the new road east toward Watson Lake and south into British Columbia. By September these same army road builders would meet workers building the highway north from Fort Nelson, connecting the middle and southern portions of the new road. A few weeks later other workers moving west from Whitehorse would break through to army crews working east from Big Delta, Alaska. This closed the remaining gap in the Alaska Highway.

Brook's Brook Named for Lieutenant Brook
Historic Milepost 829, 24.5 miles (39 km) from Teslin

The small stream of Brook's Brook was christened by American soldiers who worked on this section of the Alaska Highway in 1942. They named the brook after commanding officer in the Army Engineers, Lieutenant Brook.

Canol Pipeline Built During World War II
Johnson's Crossing, Historic Milepost 836, Alaska Highway, 31 miles (50 km) north of Teslin

Although most local people will tell you that Johnson's Crossing was named for former Teslin community leader George Johnston, the name was actually given to this spot during the construction of the Alaska Highway. Soldiers here named the camp after their commanding officer, Colonel Frank Johnson of the 93rd Engineers. Johnson headed construction crews working on the Alaska Highway and the Canol pipeline road.

The Canol pipeline from Norman Wells in the Northwest Territories to Whitehorse in the Yukon was built by the United States Army between 1942 and 1944, but the much-anticipated venture was never particularly successful. In some ways a more costly undertaking than the building of the Alaska Highway, the pipeline was declared surplus to military needs even before the end of the war.

Bridge Halts Steamer Traffic

Teslin River Bridge, Alaska Highway, 31.5 miles (51 km) north of Teslin

The Teslin River Bridge is the third longest on the Alaska Highway. It was constructed in 1942 and purposely built high enough to allow clearance for the local steamboats that regularly brought goods up the Teslin River from Whitehorse. With the building of the Alaska Highway, however, goods immediately began to arrive overland to this area. The steamboats were no longer needed. Steamboat service from Whitehorse, in fact, ended the same year the bridge was completed.

Squanga Lake Airfield Built

Historic Milepost 843, Alaska Highway, 43.5 miles (70 km) north of Teslin

An historical marker here tells of the Squanga Lake Airstrip, built in 1942 as part of the Northwest Staging Route. The name *Squanga* is from an aboriginal word for a kind of whitefish indigenous to this lake. While the lake is no longer home to an airstrip there is a small government campsite there.

Jacobson Builds Jake's Corner

Historic Milepost 866, Alaska Highway, 60 miles (97 km) north of Teslin

Several different accounts explain the origin of the name *Jake's Corner*. One story says the settlement received its name from an Indian trapper, Jake Jackson, who trapped in this area and often camped here before World War II. A more likely story is that the name dates from the building of the Alaska Highway. Captain "Jake" Jacobson was the military's commanding officer in charge of construction of this section of the Alaska Highway as well as the cutoff road from Carcross to this point on the highway. It was Jacobson, therefore, who, along with his men, created the corner. Today, Jake's Corner is known as a popular highway stop, with a gas station, motel and restaurant where, in rhubarb season, the pie alone is worth the stop.

Klondike Stampeders Spark Atlin Gold Rush
27 miles (41 km) south of Jake's Corner on Highway 7, Atlin, B.C.

Highway 7 south from Jake's Corner leads to the historic mining town of Atlin, British Columbia. Built on the shore of the stunningly beautiful Atlin Lake, the town grew up as a result of a smaller gold rush that developed during the Klondike Stampede of 1897–98.

While thousands of people were struggling over the Chilkoot and White passes intent on reaching Dawson City in the Klondike, Fritz Miller, a German immigrant, and Kenny McLaren, a Nova Scotian, spent their days prospecting creeks near Atlin Lake. By July 1898 they filed a discovery claim on Pine Creek. As word got out, a new gold rush developed, partly because of the richness of the claim but mostly because Atlin was closer than the Klondike for thousands of men and women still on the trails. Despite the lateness of the season, 3,000 people streamed into the Atlin area, creating a smaller version of boomtown Dawson City. Today, many of the buildings in the area date from the early years of the century, including the Atlin Museum, which features artifacts from the town's gold rush history.

Yukon River Becomes Highway to the Klondike
Historic Milepost 897, Yukon River Bridge, Alaska Highway, 30.5 miles (49 km) north of Jake's Corner

The Yukon River is the most important body of water in Alaska and the Yukon. Its headwaters begin upriver from the Yukon River Bridge less than 20 miles (32 km) from the Pacific Ocean. Yet, the Yukon travels well over 2,000 miles (3,219 km) before it finally reaches salt water, emptying into Norton Sound on the Bering Sea.

During the gold rush of 1897–98, thousands came north to cross the Chilkoot and White passes to get to the Yukon River, which was the shortest and cheapest route to Dawson City. Once over the Coast Mountains the stampeders stopped at the headwaters long enough to build boats to take down the Yukon to the gold fields. More expensive, but still well traveled was the all-water route to the Klondike. Stampeders taking this route needed more money, but for those who could bury the expense, and thousands could, it was possible to book passage on steamers up the coast to St. Michael on the Bering Sea at Norton Sound. From St. Michael's, passengers would take river steamers an additional 1,700 miles (2,736 km) up the Yukon River to Dawson City. In both instances, the Yukon River was the true highway to the Klondike.

Klondike Highway Connects Skagway and Dawson
Alaska and Klondike Highway junction, 37.5 miles (60 km) north of Jake's Corner

At the junction of Highway 2, today's traveler can take the Klondike Highway south to the Alaska port city of Skagway, Alaska, or follow the highway north through Whitehorse to Dawson City, the legendary gold rush capital on the mouth of the Klondike River. The Skagway portion of the highway, with portions of the road reaching well above the treeline as it crosses the Coast Mountains, opened in 1978. The road between Whitehorse and Dawson City, which follows the Yukon River most of the way, opened 20 years earlier. In 1897–98 most of the stampeders spent months getting from Skagway to Dawson City. Today, visitors can travel between the two gold rush towns over well-maintained paved roads in less than a day.

White Pass & Yukon Route Connects Yukon with Salt Water
Historic Milepost 910, Alaska Highway, 43 miles (69 km) north of Jake's Corner

The village of McCrae was born in 1900 as a stopping point on the new White Pass & Yukon Route railway. Built between 1898 and 1900, the railway track was laid over one of the most rugged mountain passes on the continent. In fact, the railway's construction was an engineering marvel that rivals the construction of the Alaska Highway itself. Much of the way through the pass the railway had to be built across solid rock. Other places required tons of gravel fill to allow track building to proceed across giant bogs.

After the gold rush years the population of the Yukon declined. During the depression, the White Pass & Yukon Route deteriorated, mostly from lack of business. Only one train a week operated during the winter months, and the railroad shut down completely after heavy snowfalls. During World War II, McCrae, where the White Pass & Yukon Route crosses the Alaska Highway, exploded with activity after a large construction camp turned the small community into a major service and supply point for highway builders.

The American army leased the White Pass & Yukon Route during the war years and perhaps saved it from bankruptcy. The army took over and built new docking and handling facilities at Skagway, upgraded the roadbed and replaced most of the White Pass & Yukon Route cars and engines with 24 new locomotives and 284 freight cars. Over 20 trains a day sometimes operated during the summer of 1943.

During the war a new telephone and telegraph line also went up between Skagway and Whitehorse, which tied Skagway into the line constructed north from Edmonton and gave the Alaska coastal community its first electronic link with the outside world.

Elliot's Navy Brings Supplies North
Historic Milepost 910, Alaska Highway, 43 miles (69 km) north of Jake's Corner

Moving equipment and supplies north during the initial stages of Alaska Highway construction created horrendous logistical problems for the American military. It was especially difficult to supply the middle-highway regiments working north and south out of Whitehorse.

Colonel William M. Hoge, overall commander of the northern section of the highway, took his problem to E.W. Elliot, a Seattle businessman who operated a few tugs and barges on the Washington coast. Elliot immediately went to work acquiring additional craft for his fleet. Soon, in addition to more tugs and barges, he owned a freighter, several pleasure yachts and even a schooner that he put to work ferrying highway supplies and equipment north on the inside passage to Alaska. By May 1942, "Elliot's Navy" had freighted most of Hoge's supplies north to Skagway, where they were shipped over the White Pass & Yukon Route railway to Carcross, McCrae and Whitehorse.

Miles Canyon Sinks Stampeders
Alaska Highway, 45 miles (72 km) north of Jake's Corner, right-hand turn at camera viewpoint sign, follow road to right-hand fork, then .5 miles (.8 km) to parking lot

Miles Canyon and the Whitehorse Rapids just below it were the two most dangerous spots on the Yukon River for stampeders during the gold rush of 1897–98. In the summer of 1898, after more than 150 boats had been wrecked and several argonauts had lost their lives, the North-West Mounted Police imposed a regulation that stipulated only sea-worthy boats with competent pilots were allowed to pass through the canyon. From this time on, many of the stampeders carried their boats and tons of equipment and supplies around the canyon and rapids. Others hired experienced oarsmen to take them through.

A persistent gold rush legend tells that the young Jack London, soon to be the most famous writer of the Yukon, was for a time a commercial pilot at Miles Canyon. The story maintains that London made several thousand dollars as a Yukon boatsmen. In fact, he piloted only one boat besides his own through the waters of the canyon, and that one boat belonged to a friend who paid the former sailor nothing for his trouble. A short time after the Mounties imposed their regulations, a tramway was built around the canyon by some enterprising gold seeker. After that, almost no one chanced losing a boat, supplies or their lives to the raging waters of the canyon.

Railroad, Highway and Steamboats Bring Prominence to Whitehorse
Alaska Highway, Whitehorse

Today's city of Whitehorse is located at what was the head of Whitehorse Rapids, a stopping-off place for miners after passing through Miles Canyon. The name was in common use by the late 1880s. The name may have had something to do with how the white-water rapids here resemble the mane of a white horse.

From its origins, Whitehorse has been a community built around transportation. In the early years, it grew because it was the practical limit for steamboat traffic moving upstream on the Yukon River. Because of this location, the White Pass & Yukon

Route railway chose Whitehorse as its northern terminus. Then, because of the railroad, the Alaska Highway was routed through Whitehorse during World War II. And because of the highway, Whitehorse became the most important town in the Yukon, supplanting Dawson City for this honor. After 1953, when the territorial capital was moved from Dawson to Whitehorse, the town grew even more.

Today, many of Whitehorse's pioneer buildings are still in use. Visitors can take historical walking tours leaving from Donnenworth House, which was originally built by "Hobo Bill" Donneworth and had a tent attached to the back of it. Eventually, the house was expanded and the tent removed.

Other buildings of historical interest in Whitehorse include the White Pass and Yukon Route railway depot. Some of Whitehorse's more unusual buildings include a number of multi-level log structures scattered throughout the city, which date from the 1940s, when construction of the Alaska Highway created a housing shortage in Whitehorse. Martin Berrigna, who came to the Yukon during the Klondike Gold Rush, built the cabins as rental units. Each level of his log skyscrapers contained a separate apartment. Many are still in use today.

Steamboats Paddle Yukon

SS Klondike *National Historic Site, next to the Robert Campbell Bridge, Whitehorse*

The steamboat SS *Klondike* once plied the waters of the Yukon River. Today, after being refurbished by Parks Canada, the old sternwheeler sits at the edge of the river in Whitehorse, operating as a museum for Yukon visitors. Tours of the craft are scheduled every half hour and a film on the history of riverboat traffic on the Yukon is shown daily in an adjacent tent theater.

Steamdriven riverboats plied the waters of the Yukon for nearly a century before highways and dependable air service finally put an end to them in the early 1950s. Two ships on the river actually bore the name SS *Klondike*. The first was built in 1929 in Whitehorse. At the time it was the largest riverboat on the Yukon.

The first SS *Klondike* was destroyed after it hit a rock and sank near Hootalinqua in 1936. Pieces of the wreckage can still be found along the riverbank today. The second SS *Klondike*— the same size as the first—was built the following year. The new ship worked the river until 1952, when most of the ore and supplies between Dawson, Mayo and Whitehorse began going by truck over the new highways. For a time the SS *Klondike* attempted to run as a tourist boat on the Yukon River, but it never made enough money to turn a profit for the owners. The ship made its last trip in the summer of 1955. In 1966 it was moved through downtown Whitehorse to its present location pulled by bulldozers across 8 tons (7.25 tonnes) of Palmolive soap.

Canadian Army Takes Control of Alaska Highway
The Yukon Transportation Museum, Alaska Highway, Whitehorse

Three cairns near the Yukon Transportation Museum's front door commemorate the construction of the Alaska Highway and its eventual control by the Canadian army and, later, civilian authorities. In a ceremony in Whitehorse on April 1, 1946, the 1,220-mile (1,963-km) Canadian section of the Alaska Highway was formally turned over to the Canadian army by American officials. The terms of the transfer had been spelled out in the original agreement between Canada and the United States in early 1942.

This agreement, made during the first terrible months of the war, called for the United States to build a road across northwestern Canada at U.S. expense. The road was to be used and controlled by the American army during the war, but within six months of the war's end it was to be returned to Canada. At the time of the agreement, the exigencies of the war muted most criticism of the proposed highway within Canada—although a few nationalists suggested the American military presence along the highway was only a first step in the eventual takeover of the northwest by the United States.

As it turned out, not only was the road returned to Canada immediately after the war, but the Americans actually tried to give it back while the war was still in progress. At the time, though, the Canadian government wouldn't take it. The highway would have been too great a financial burden. The higher-than-anticipated costs, in fact, explained why the Americans became so anxious to give it back.

Even at the end of the war, the Alaska Highway was not built to the standards promised in the initial agreement between the two countries. Long before the road north was due to be finished in the autumn of 1943, the fortunes of war with Japan had changed. A major Japanese invasion was no longer deemed a real threat. By the time the United States Public Roads Administration (PRA) took over the job of upgrading the pioneer road in the autumn of 1942, the Alaska Highway was not seen as a military priority.

Friction between the PRA and the army occurred regularly as the PRA's mission to upgrade the highway to civilian standards came into conflict with the army's desire to get the job finished as quickly and inexpensively as possible. And during the war, when arguments arose between the PRA and the military, the army always got its way. By the end of 1943, money for the construction of the Alaska Highway essentially ran out. The cost had already surpassed $135 million or more than $66,000 a mile. After that, work centered on routine maintenance and upgrading needed to ensure the road remained open.

Despite these problems, rebuilding and paving were completed in Alaska by the early 1960s, though the northern climate kept the road from living up to southern standards. Frost heaves and pot holes often made the Alaskan portion of the highway seem worse than the gravel on the Canadian side. In following years the highway in Alaska was repaved several times. By the 1980s the Alaska section had become comparable to most southern highways carrying similar traffic loads.

Upgrading the Canadian portion of the highway became a more daunting task. When the Canadian army took over the Canadian section of the road in 1946, the Alaska Highway was essentially as it had been at the end of 1943—except that the temporary log bridges had aged and were even closer to collapse. There was, of course, no military reason for the Canadian army to take over the highway. Their expertise was in building temporary military roads, not civilian highways. On the surface, it made more sense to turn control of the Canadian part of the highway over to the two governments who shared the road, the Yukon Territory and the province of British Columbia, just as the American section of the road had been turned over to the state of Alaska.

The tiny territorial government of the Yukon, however, lacked the resources to maintain the road, let alone improve it. The British Columbia government had no desire to take on the expense either. They had already built a road to connect Prince George with the Alaska Highway. If the federal government had incurred a wartime obligation to the United States to take over the road, that, so far as British Columbia was concerned, was a federal problem, even though the province would reap the benefits of the road without having to pay a cent.

In 1946, the job of reconstructing the deteriorating Canadian section of the highway fell to the Northwest Highway System wing of the Royal Canadian Engineers. Canadians along the highway wanted the road improved, but in the years immediately after the war the federal government chose to undertake only the minimum amount of work necessary to keep the road open.

Nevertheless, a slow process of rebuilding bridges and whole sections of the highway began. The road in the western

A four-ton truck loaded with beer is being winched out of the Tahkini River in 1942. The beer was destined for 4th of July celebrations at a nearby construction camp.

Yukon between Kluane Lake and the border was a particular source of trouble. Bridges such as the Slims and White spanned glacial rivers prone to flooding and course changes. The 300-mile (483-km) stretch of highway north of Fort Nelson was also troublesome, with numerous washouts every spring closing whole sections of the highway for days at a time. By 1964, however, the Royal Canadian Engineers had built more than 100 new bridges.

The British Columbia government took over the first 83 miles (134 km) of paved and improved road in the early 1960s. Then, exactly 18 years to the day after the Canadian army assumed control of the road, it was transferred to the civilian Department of Public Works. The Canadian section of the Alaska Highway was still in the hands of the federal government, but promoters felt the long overdue improvements to the road, in the form of massive rebuilding, would finally take place.

Instead of beginning immediately to rebuild the highway, however, the federal government postponed action by commissioning a study, and to the anger of highway promoters on both sides of the border, the Stanford Research Institute reported that there was no economic justification for paving or even upgrading the entire highway.

Political pressure did push ahead the construction of some major bridges, and the Department of Public Works undertook upgrading. Some paving around towns even took place, as did substantial rebuilding of parts of the southern third of the highway, where the road was used most. But the massive upgrading that promoters had been calling for was dropped in favor of gradual improvements along selected sections of the highway.

By the late 1960s several American politicians were calling for joint Canadian and American programs to upgrade and pave the highway on the Canadian side of the border. Since much of the traffic along the highway was from the United States, and because it provided the only land link to Alaska, Alaskans, particularly, called for some kind of joint venture. In 1970 the United States Congress authorized the president to negotiate a deal with the Canadian government to improve some sections of the highway.

In 1972 the Yukon Territorial government took over maintenance of the Yukon section of the highway, but British Columbia still balked at taking over its share of the road. From its point of view, the situation was ideal. The federal government paid for the highway while the province collected the gasoline taxes along its route.

The U.S. government eventually approached Canada with a plan to pave and upgrade the highway from the Alaska border to Haines Junction in the western Yukon. The Haines Highway, from Haines Junction to Haines, Alaska, on the Pacific Coast was also to be paved. The motive for the American plan was simple: Alaska State Ferries could dock at Haines, and the improved road would offer travelers better access to the interior.

Canadians used this section of highway the least, so it was of minimal concern to the Canadian government. But with American dollars, construction began in 1977. Before the entire plan could be worked out, however, money for the project dried up in the budget cuts of the 1980s. Once more, work on the highway slowed to a more gradual pace. Today, although upgrading of the highway continues, the entire route from Dawson Creek to Fairbanks has finally been paved. Overall, the highway is built now to a standard equal to roads throughout North America.

Whitehorse Airport Built on Clear-Cut
Whitehorse Airport, Alaska Highway, Whitehorse

The first airplanes to fly in the Yukon were four de Havilland biplanes belonging to the United States Army Air Corps. They made a stopover at Whitehorse in 1920 on a flight between Mineola, New York, and Nome, Alaska. Mike Cyr cleared a field outside of Whitehorse especially for the landing. He cut a swath of trees with a crosscut saw, leaving the stumps flush with the ground in an area big enough for the planes to land. This field eventually became part of today's Whitehorse Airport.

Although air travel became relatively common in the Yukon during the late 1920s and 1930s, the most formidable increase in air transportation came during and after World War II, when the string of air bases in the Northwest Staging Route brought military aircraft through the North on a daily basis. After the war, surplus military planes and former military pilots came north because the northwest wilderness was especially well suited to air travel.

Pilots had to be a courageous lot. Lakes and rivers were often substitutes for air strips. Planes were rigged with pontoons in the summers and skis in the winter. Flying conditions, especially in the dark cold winter months could be treacherous. Travel was also hampered because there were few roads or other obvious landmarks that could be used to guide pilots into the most isolated regions. Plane crashes were common and often fatal.

Air mail service began in the Yukon in 1927, when planes from Whitehorse flew north to Dawson and threw their mailbags out their window from the sky. Eventually, this service became more routine and official stops for mail delivery appeared. In 1950, airplanes took over the last dog-sled mail route between Dawson City and Eagle, Alaska, completing the transformation of Yukon life by aircraft.

Old Dawson Trail Connects Whitehorse and Dawson
Historic Milepost 937, Alaska Highway, 6 miles (10 km) west of Whitehorse

The Dawson, or Overland, Trail crosses the Takhini River at this point, known as Yukon Crossing. The Dawson Trail came into regular use during the winter of 1901–02 and continued to be used until the opening of the Mayo–Dawson Road in 1950. It was used almost exclusively during the winter months, when regular stage service was available over the trail and travel on the river ice was rough and unpredictable. During the summer, steamboats provided transportation between Dawson and the northern terminus of the White Pass & Yukon Route railway at Whitehorse.

Slim Williams Becomes First to Drive Alaska Highway
Historic Milepost 937, Alaska Highway, 6 miles (10 km) west of Whitehorse

In 1932, when the Alaska Highway was still only a dream, a veteran prospector named Slim Williams, in an argument over the quality of his dogs, boasted that he would drive his team all the way to the Century of Progress Fair in Chicago, Illinois. News of Williams' promise was picked up by Alaska newspapers, leaving the aging sourdough with no honorable way out of his boast, except to undertake the long journey.

Advocates of a highway connecting Alaska with the United States hit upon the idea of Williams' proposed dog-mushing adventure as a way to promote their cause. Donald MacDonald, one of Alaska's leading highway proponents, sent Williams money to make the trip and a letter of introduction to Anthony Diamond, the Alaska territorial representative in Congress. When Williams said he was only going to Chicago, not Washington, MacDonald taunted him with the notion that Washington was only a few hundred miles farther, and if he went, Williams might even get to meet the president.

Williams left Copper Center in Alaska on November 21, when the temperature was −40°. He made good time mushing north through Chicken to Fortymile in the Yukon Territory and then up the Yukon River to Dawson City. From Dawson, Williams traveled along the old Dawson Trail, passing this point on today's Alaska Highway on his way into Whitehorse.

Once past Whitehorse, though, Williams ran into repeated difficulties. Instead of following the route of today's Alaska Highway, he traveled south over a route advocated by MacDonald and other early promoters of the highway. This took Williams along the eastern side of the Coast Mountains to Telegraph Creek in British Columbia and then on to Hazelton, near the southern tip of southeast Alaska.

During this 800-mile (1,287-km) stretch Williams mushed through snow that was often so deep he had to make a trail for his dogs before they could get through. Some days, he was only able to travel a mile or two. Other times he had to deal with sickness and snow blindness. Once, he nearly drowned when his sled went through a weak spot in river ice.

Finally, on May 15, Williams arrived at a Mountie's cabin outside of Hazelton. He stopped here to rest for a few days, and after rigging his sled with axles and wheels to cross the now snowless landscape, he continued south. By the time Williams reached the United States border, news of his exploit had been picked up by radio and newspaper reporters. Suddenly, the old sourdough found himself a celebrity. In the warm southern climate, he drove his dogs only at night, when it was cooler and there was less traffic.

Williams finally reached Chicago on September 16. A police escort took him down Michigan Avenue. After six weeks at the fair, where Williams had a tent pitched next to the Alaska exhibit, he left for Washington. This leg of the trip took another month, but when he got there, Williams did, indeed, get to meet President Roosevelt. The president asked him if building a road to Alaska was possible. Williams replied that he'd already traveled it.

Forest Fires Ravage Yukon in 1958
Interpretive Signs, Alaska Highway, 21 miles (34 km) west of Whitehorse

---

More than 1.5 million acres (607,050 ha) of Yukon forest burned in this area in 1958. That summer, a drought had engulfed the entire northwest. Even the town of Whitehorse was threatened as the fire approached the city limits before being brought under control. Only now, after nearly 40 years, are the young trees beginning to look like a forest again.

Champagne Celebration on the Dalton Trail
Historic Milepost 974, Champagne, Alaska Highway, 49 miles (79 km) west of Whitehorse

---

According to an old story, Champagne received its name from a group of cowboys who celebrated here with a bottle of French champagne in 1898. At that time, the place was merely a campsite at the end of the first leg of Jack Dalton's trail from Haines Mission, on the Alaska coast, to Fort Selkirk, south of Dawson City. The cowboys were celebrating the successful completion of that part of their journey with champagne pilfered from other supplies being sent north.

When Jack Dalton came to the area in 1891 the trail that would bear his name was a traditional Chilkoot Indian route from the coast. He established and successfully maintained the trail during the Klondike Gold Rush, charging fees to anyone who wanted to use it to reach Dawson City. Since the Dalton Trail was the best trail to the Klondike for pack animals and livestock, most of the early cattle and sheep to arrive in the Klondike came over this route, with a toll charged for each animal brought into the country.

In 1902 "Shorty" Chambers built a trading post at Champagne. When the Kluane Gold Rush occurred the following year, a wagon road was built between Whitehorse and Kluane Lake, with Champagne becoming an important supply point along the route.

Sam McGee Builds Canyon Creek Bridge
Historic Milepost 996, Alaska Highway, 22 miles (35 km) west of Champagne

Aishihik River was once known as Canyon Creek. In 1904, Sam McGee and a partner in a roadhouse venture built a log bridge across the stream. This bridge became an important link on the wagon road connecting Whitehorse to Silver City on Kluane Lake. Though the bridge has since been replaced several times, the Yukon government rebuilt Sam McGee's original bridge in 1987, and it can be seen north of the highway at this point.

Sam McGee became famous, however, not as a bridge builder but as the title character in Robert Service's famous poem "The Cremation of Sam McGee." Service didn't know Sam McGee when he wrote the poem, but he had heard of him. When he sat down to write a tale about a cremation on the shore of Lake Laberge, he decided McGee's name had just the right ring to fit his new verse. Later, while Service was working as a cashier in a bank in Dawson City, Sam McGee walked in and introduced himself to the poet who had appropriated his name.

Alaska Highway Passes Ancient Indian Camp
Alaska Highway, Aishihik River

An ancient Indian camp is located near the place where today's highway crosses the Aishihik River. Although the area is forested now, the camp originally overlooked grasslands covering what had earlier been the bottom of glacial Lake Champagne. Archaeologists have excavated several layers of material including stone spearheads, microblades and several large bison bones. These artifacts suggest humans—perhaps ancestors of today's Athabascan people—have camped at this spot for at least 8,000 years.

A mile (1.6 km) east of the Aishihik River and Historic Mile-post 996, a turnoff on the Aishihik Road leads to today's Indian community of Aishihik. Along the way, the road passes near Otter Falls, famous for a time because its picture was painted on an earlier version of the Canadian five-dollar bill.

Hunting by Soldiers Leads to Kluane National Park
Alaska Highway, Haines Junction, 41 miles (66 km) west of Champagne

Kluane National Park began as Kluane Game Sanctuary during World War II, when local native people and white residents became concerned about the slaughter of wildlife by army personnel working in the area on the Alaska Highway. Hunting was a popular activity for the soldiers. Alberta and the Yukon allowed American soldiers stationed within their borders to acquire resident hunting licenses. British Columbia and Alaska, somewhat ironically, did not.

In 1943 a large tract of land was set aside in the Kluane Lake area as a game preserve. The reserve was declared a formal park in 1972, and in 1976 formal national park boundaries were established on the west side of the Alaska Highway and the Haines Road. This vast area includes, some say, the world's most beautiful mountains. It is home to grizzly bear and dall sheep, some of the world's greatest glaciers and some of the most diverse plant life on the continent. In 1980, Kluane National Park and adjoining Wrangell–St. Elias National Park in Alaska became a joint UNESCO World Heritage Site.

Haines Road Built During World War II
Historic Milepost 1016, Alaska Highway, Haines Junction, 41.5 miles (67 km) west of Champagne

In 1942 Haines Junction became an important construction camp for builders of the Alaska Highway. In addition to the work carried out on the highway, crews also built a connecting road from Haines Junction to the coast at Haines, Alaska. Today's Haines Road loosely follows the old Dalton Trail from Haines over the mountains. Near Dezadeash Lake, it diverts from the old trail as it continues to the Alaska Highway at Haines Junction.

Interpretive displays and historical photographs can be seen at the visitor information center in Haines Junction. Roadside historical markers can also be found at the junction of the Haines and Alaska highways. In addition to the Alaska Highway Anniversary historical marker in Haines Junction—which describes the construction of the road to Haines, Alaska—another set of historical panels describing the building of the Haines Road can be found 102 miles (164 km) south of the Alaska Highway on a turnout along the Haines Road.

Side Trip from Haines Junction: Haines Road

Klukshu Indian Village Displays Traditional Salmon Fishing
40 miles (64 km) south of Haines Junction, Haines Road, Klukshu

Visitors to this historic native fishing camp can view traditional methods of catching and processing salmon along the Klukshu River. *Klukshu* is a Tlingit word meaning "coho place." Interpretive signs, displays of Indian artifacts (including fish traps and drying racks) and contemporary native crafts can be found here.

Jack Dalton Forges Trail
Dalton Post, 52 miles (84 km) south of Haines Junction, Haines Road

The Dalton Trail, opened by Jack Dalton in 1896, incorporated several Indian trails that had been used by Chilkat and other Indians for centuries. It led from Haines Mission in Alaska through the town of Champagne in the Yukon to the gold fields farther north. The Tlingit Indians called the trail over the mountains the Grease Trail because of the significant role that eulachon, or candlefish, oil played in their trade with Indians from the interior.

Fifty-two miles (84 km) south of Haines Junction, a turnoff on a short winding mountain road leads to a group of abandoned log buildings, which were originally part of Dalton Post, a stopping point on the Dalton Trail. Jack Dalton, a thickset frontiersman from Oklahoma, who first came north in 1890, established Dalton Post in 1893 or 1894. In addition to the stopping place here, Dalton used the nearby area to graze and winter pack horses. For a time in 1898, he operated a pony express service between Haines Mission and Fort Selkirk, upriver from Dawson City. Between 1897 and 1904, a North-West Mounted Police detachment operated at Dalton Post.

Most of the livestock brought to the Klondike during the gold rush came in over Dalton's trail for a fee. In 1898 alone, 2,000 head of cattle arrived over this route. In addition to Jack Dalton's, several other tolls were set up—for roads, bridges and other shortcuts—along the various routes to the Klondike. But Jack Dalton's was the only toll on any of the routes that managed to be collected consistently throughout the gold rush. Dalton's toll was a success because he patrolled his trail with a six-gun and rifle, threatening to shoot anyone who didn't pay. No one questioned Dalton's resolve. It was well known that prior to the start of the gold rush he had shot and killed at least one man who allegedly had tried to set the Chilkat against him, an action that Dalton and others who knew of Chilkat ferocity saw as nothing less than attempted murder.

Historical Stops in Haines, Alaska
151 miles (243 km) south of Haines Junction, Haines Road

Several stops of historical interest can be found 151 miles (243 km) south of the Alaska Highway at Haines, Alaska. The Sheldon Museum and Cultural Center, established in 1924, includes Chilkat art and artifacts, gold rush memorabilia and other local history displays. Fort William H. Seward dates from the early years of the 20th century, when it was the regimental headquarters for the United States Army in Alaska.

In the years before the outbreak of World War II, Fort Seward was the only army base in Alaska. Today, most of the buildings have become private residences and businesses. The area, though, has been designated an historic site. The Alaska Indian Arts and Totem Village here features Chilkat cultural displays. The American Bald Eagle Foundation Headquarters and Natural History Museum is also located in Haines.

Returning to the Alaska Highway at Haines Junction

Mackintosh Trading Post at Bear Creek
Mackintosh Lodge, Historic Milepost 1022, Alaska Highway, 6.5 miles (10.5 km) north of Haines Junction

Originally called the Bear Creek Roadhouse, the Mackintosh Trading Post was built in 1904 by an early trader named Beauchamp. He operated it as a roadhouse on the Whitehorse to Kluane Lake wagon road. By the time American soldiers arrived here in 1942 to work on the Alaska Highway, Dorothy Mackintosh, the widow of a Mounted Policeman, was running the post, which she continued to do until the 1950s.

Southern Tutchone Name Kluane Lake
Alaska Highway, 35 miles (56 km) north of Haines Junction

Southern Tutchone people, who have lived in the Kluane Lake area for generations, gave the lake here the name *Kluane,* which means "Big Fish Lake." It was a prominent fishing place for native people before the arrival of Europeans in the 19th century.

The longest continuously inhabited region on the North American continent can be found in the interior of Alaska and the Yukon. The first North Americans arrived here over a land bridge from Asia perhaps 30,000 years ago. Although much of Alaska and the Yukon of that time remained free of glaciers, the way south was blocked by ice for several thousand years. Eventually, a path through the glaciers opened, and the settlement of the rest of North and South America began.

For centuries, the interior region of Alaska and the Yukon has been inhabited by Athabascan-speaking people: the Tutchone, Han, Kutchin, Tanacross, Tanana and others. Despite many differences, the Athabascan groups have had much more in common than just their languages. At the time of European arrival in North America, the Athabascans of Alaska and Yukon dressed in similar fashion, with caribou, moose and rabbit skins used to make much of their clothing. Porcupine quills and shell beads were used for decoration. Ear-rings and necklaces were used by both men and women.

Winter shelters differed from summer ones. In winter, one or more families would live in a wigwam-style pole house covered with moss and soil. In summer, they lived in similarly shaped skin-covered shelters, which were portable.

During the summer months, the Athabascans frequently traveled on the rivers and streams in birch canoes, moosehide skiffs and other types of boats. In winter, they used snowshoes and sleds. Sometimes—such as during the autumn caribou hunts—the Athabascans lived and hunted communally. Other times, they separated into family units. In addition to hunting the meat of land animals, the Athabascans also were great fishermen. Salmon and other fish made up an important part of their diet.

Silver City Born in Gold Rush
Historic Milepost 1053, Alaska Highway, 35.5 miles (57 km) north of Haines Junction

Ruins of the old mining town of Silver City can be found three miles (five km) along the side road north of this point. The Kluane Gold Rush began in the summer of 1903, when Tagish Charlie, one of the original discoverers of the Klondike gold fields, discovered gold on Fourth of July Creek near Kluane Lake. At this time prospectors were spread throughout Alaska and the Yukon in the aftermath of the Klondike Gold Rush of 1897–98, looking for new Eldoradoes of their own. By the end of the year, more than 2,000 claims had been staked in the Kluane region. The community of Silver City sprang up on the lake at the outlet of Silver Creek.

The next year a wagon road from Whitehorse was cut following Indian trails long used by the southern Tutchone. Mining in the area never proved particularly profitable, however, and by 1925 the town's population had dwindled to only one resident. In 1942 Silver City was briefly brought back to life when the United States Army used the old mining town as a site for a construction camp. Today, the dilapidated buildings of Silver City, some in relatively sturdy condition, others with sagging roofs and crumbling walls, have, once more, become part of a ghost town.

Gold Rush Leads Horse to River and Prospector to Grave
Slim's River Bridge, Alaska Highway, 43 miles (69 km) north of Haines Junction

Slim's River gets its name from a miner's packhorse that drowned while crossing the river during the 1903 Kluane Gold Rush. A mile (.6 km) north of the river, the Sheep Mountain Visitor Information Centre offers interpretive programs and information about Kluane National Park. On the hillside above the center, a small white cross marks the gravesite of Alexander Clark Fisher, who came to the area in the aftermath of the short-lived Kluane Gold Rush. Fisher was a prospector, but he stayed in the area even when the gold diggings had apparently run their course. Fisher continued to work the streams near Slim's River until his death in 1941. He was buried near his cabin, but the following year, surveyors determined that the new Alcan Highway should go right through the cabin and over the gravesite. Despite protests from local people the grave was moved to the spot next to the highway where Fisher rests today. The white cross is a memorial of sorts to all early prospectors in the Yukon.

Alaska Highway Completed at Soldier's Summit
Historic Milepost 1061, Soldier's Summit, Alaska Highway, 46 miles (74 km) north of Haines Junction

Construction crew near Soldier's Summit on Kluane Lake in 1942.

At this spot, where today's highway winds along the shores of Kluane Lake, a well-marked trail leads up the ridge at the side of the road. At the top of the trail, with Kluane Range looming above them, visitors will find a plaque marking the site where Canadian and American representatives held a ribbon-cutting ceremony on November 20, 1942, to officially open the Alaska Highway. The road had taken only eight months to build, but it was a pioneer highway only, a tote road cut through the wilderness. The real highway would be built in the months and years to come. This little stretch of trail though, with its impressive views of the lake and Ruby Mountains beyond, is one of the few remaining segments of the original road, a short stretch of trail cut through the wilderness, where, on a cold November day almost half a century ago, officials declared the Alaska Highway open for traffic.

View of Kluane Lake at Kluane Flats in 1942, with U.S. Army construction camp in center of photo.

Storm Destroys Buildings on Destruction Bay
Historic Milepost 1083, Alaska Highway, Destruction Bay, 66 miles (106 km) north of Haines Junction

Destruction Bay was one of more than a dozen towns born as relay stations during the construction of the Alaska Highway. After the initial construction of the highway it was necessary to keep military and construction supplies moving nonstop in both directions along the new road. Relay stations, spaced every 100 miles (161 km), were designed to spell off truck drivers and repair vehicles. They were sizable camps with repair shops and refueling facilities. Hot meals were served 24 hours a day. The station received its name after a storm in the early days of construction destroyed buildings and supplies here.

U.S. Army Comes to Burwash Landing
Historic Milepost 1093, Burwash Landing, Alaska Highway, 76.5 miles (123 km) north of Haines Junction

Burwash Landing seemed to be an oasis in the wilderness for the United States Army troops when they arrived here during the building of the Alaska Highway in 1942. At Burwash, troops, who for months had known nothing but camp life, suddenly came upon an established community. There were well-tended gardens, horses and cattle, fresh milk, a sawmill and a well-stocked trading post.

Burwash had been established nearly 40 years earlier, during the Kluane Gold Rush. Eugene and Louis Jacquot first settled here when they opened a trading post in 1904. After the gold rush ended, the brothers went on to establish a big-game guiding business. The Jacquot brothers called the community that grew here Burwash Landing in honor of their friend Lachlin Taylor Burwash, the mining recorder at Silver City. The name *Jacquot Post* had also been used until the building of the highway when the original name became official.

Kluane Museum Displays Dog
Kluane Museum, Alaska Highway, Burwash Landing

Perhaps the best northern wildlife exhibit in the Yukon, the Kluane Museum was started in the 1960s by local people who wanted to show what life was like here before the highway. The present building was constructed in the 1970s and then renovated in 1988, with the major redevelopment completed in 1992. Wildlife displays predominate, but there are also several exhibits focusing on aboriginal history and culture.

In front of the museum, along with other displays, is what appears to be a life-sized fiberglass dog. The fiberglass is only a coating, however. A real dog that once belonged to Catholic missionary Father Huyjberg is underneath. Huyjberg was instrumental in founding the Burwash Museum, and after the death of a favorite dog, he had the animal stuffed and put on display next to a fiberglass trapper. So far as is known, the trapper's fiberglass coating does not hide the body of any former friend of Father Huyjberg.

Father Huyjberg came to Burwash Landing in the 1960s to work at the Catholic mission that had been established by Father Eusebe Morisset during World War II. Morisset was an Oblate missionary who served as auxiliary chaplin with the United States Army during the building of the Alaska Highway. He stayed on in Burwash to open the church located behind and across the road from the museum. The log building is a converted United States Army mess hall and cabin, donated by the army after the closure of the Duke River Construction Camp.

Memorial Erected to Lieutenant Roland Small
Historic Milepost 1117, Alaska Highway, 21.5 miles (35 km) north of Burwash Landing

The soldiers who built the Alaska Highway never faced enemy fire. Nevertheless, many of them lost their lives accidentally during the road's construction. Lieutenant Roland Small was one of them. He died in a jeep accident near this point on August 9, 1942. Small was born in Canada in 1913, earned a degree in civil engineering at New York City College and worked with the 18th Engineers on the Alaska Highway between Whitehorse and the Alaska border. He was buried in Whitehorse, but members of his platoon erected a monument here. Later, the government of the Yukon placed an historical marker on the site.

Almost all the soldiers who were killed during the construction of the Alaska Highway died in vehicle accidents or drowned in lakes and rivers along the route. Truck and equipment accidents accounted for most of the deaths. Enlisted men referred to the army's big four-wheel-drive trucks as "widow-makers" because they frequently went off the road, often causing death or injury to driver and passengers. Once one of these trucks started to slide it was reported that there was relatively little a driver could do to keep the vehicle on the road. The hard winters of the North were also responsible for casualties along the highway. Although deaths from freezing were few, many soldiers took the scars of frostbitten fingers and toes home with them.

Alaska Highway Builders Face Added Difficulties
South side of Donjek River Bridge, Alaska Highway, 38 miles (61 km) north of Burwash Landing

---

U.S. Army builds first Donjek River Bridge near Kluane Lake in 1942.

U.S. Army jeep stuck in mud near Edith Creek in 1942.

Glacial rivers like the Donjek created problems for engineers and builders of the Alaska Highway in the 1940s. After heavy rainfall, or during times of fast glacial melt, rivers flood and deposit huge quantities of glacial silt when the waters recede. Sometimes the glacial material even alters the paths of the rivers, leaving bridges crossing dry land. This is, in fact, what happened to the original bridge across the Donjek River.

Permafrost was another major problem encountered by highway construction crews in this area. Swamps and muskeg lie only a few feet above the permafrost. When the road was cut through the area, thick layers of insulating material were removed to make a road bed. This quickly thawed the natural bed of permafrost, turning long stretches of the road into muck within a few hours. Entire sections of the highway that had appeared stable turned into mud holes so deep that vehicles could sink out of sight. Eventually, engineers learned to build roadbeds over the permafrost and its insulating cover.

Trail to Alaska Gold Rush Short-Lived
Alaska Highway, 112 miles (180 km) north of Burwash Landing

An historical marker here tells of a crude trail through this area used briefly during the Chisana Gold Rush of 1913. This relatively minor gold rush brought thousands of stampeders into eastern Alaska, particularly from the Tanana River areas, but many also came from the Yukon, particularly from the Klondike region. The Chisana Trail followed Beaver Creek south and west to the Chisana District in Alaska, about 50 miles (81 km) west of the Yukon border in the Nitzotin Mountains. To the dismay of the stampeders, the Chisana Gold Rush proved to be short-lived. The communities that were so quickly established in the region were abandoned almost as fast as they had been built. Prospectors went on to other diggings in Alaska and the Yukon, many of them once again taking the trail along Beaver Creek and heading back to the Klondike. Today, much of the old gold fields of the Chisana lie enclosed in the 730,000-acre (295,431 ha) Tetlin Wildlife Refuge.

Indian Village Records Coldest Temperature in Canada
Snag turnoff, Alaska Highway, 94 miles (151 km) north of Burwash Landing

The turnoff here leads to an abandoned airfield and an Indian village named Snag, at the mouth of Snag Creek on the White River. Snag Creek was named in 1899 by two United States government surveyors because of the difficulty they had getting through the underbrush along its banks. The Canadian government established an emergency airstrip and weather station near the mouth of the river in 1942.

Snag has the dubious distinction of holding the lowest official temperature ever recorded in North America. On February 7, 1949, the temperature here dropped to a chilling –81°. Even islands in the high arctic have never recorded temperatures so low. At the time, weather station thermometers weren't even calibrated below –80°. Men at the Snag station reported that anyone who went outside left long trails of ice hanging in midair as he walked. The men threw a bowl of water into the air and watched it fall to the ground as tiny round ice pellets. When smashed, thin sheets of ice sounded exactly like breaking glass. Metal snapped apart like frozen plastic. Rubber became hard as concrete and the dogs' leather harness, instead of bending, would snap if twisted.

Historic Meeting at Beaver Creek
Historic Milepost 1202, Alaska Highway, 107 miles (172 km) north of Burwash Landing

---

On October 29, 1942, twenty miles (32 km) east of the Alaska–Yukon border near Beaver Creek, bulldozer driver Refine Sims, Jr., cutting the road south, pushed through the trees at the head of a crew working from Alaska. Suddenly, Sims saw trees falling toward him. Sims jammed his bulldozer into reverse and waited as another bulldozer burst through the forest. The driver, Alfred Jalufka, a Texan, had been working at the head of a crew cutting the road north.

Jalufka stopped his bulldozer momentarily. Then the two men drove slowly forward, parked their machines nose to nose, jumped down and shook hands. With this meeting of two enlisted men—one from a northern Black ghetto, the other from Texas ranching country—the Alaska Highway had finally been completed. It stretched through more than 1,600 miles (2,575 km) of wilderness from Dawson Creek, British Columbia, to Fairbanks, Alaska.

Details of the road's completion did not immediately reach the rest of North America. The news wasn't classified information, but as a war measure, it was decided to keep the matter of the highway's opening low key. The first news broadcast to tell of the event, in fact, was carried by Japanese radio. According to that report, the new road was a great thing for Japan because it would allow Japanese Imperial Forces easier access to the rest of North America.

After the meeting at Beaver Creek it was finally possible, at least in theory, to drive from southern Canada and the United States all the way to Alaska, and to drive from Alaska into Canada. A Canadian customs station checkpoint was established at Beaver Creek and a community grew up around the site. The Canadian customs station remained here until 1983, when it was moved to a site just north of town.

Twenty-Foot (Six-Meter) Swath Cut from Arctic Ocean to Mt. St. Elias

Historic Milepost 1221, Yukon–Alaska border, Alaska Highway, 22 miles (35 km) north of Beaver Creek

The international border is marked by a 20-foot (6-M) swath cut rhough the forest along the 141st Meridian. The path was first cut by surveyors between 1904 and 1920. It runs for 600 miles (966 km) from the Arctic Ocean to Mt. St. Elias in the Wrangell Mountains. The Canada–U.S. Boundary Commission keep the strip clear.

For several years the Alaska–Yukon border was in dispute. Because of a 19th-century treaty between Russia and Great Britain, the 141st Meridian was accepted as the boundary along the interior portions of the territories. Few people, though, knew exactly where the boundary was until the surveyors arrived in 1904.

The border along the southeastern Alaska Panhandle was a more controversial matter. Canadians claimed portions of the territory all the way to the Pacific. The United States, for its part, claimed land 20 miles (32 km) inside the present Canadian border, as far as Bennett Lake. During the Klondike Gold Rush the North-West Mounted Police were on the scene first and established posts at the summits of the mountain passes, securing Canadian sovereignty at least that far. While the United States did not challenge the Red Coat position, they still claimed territory in present-day British Columbia. The matter was finally settled in 1904 in a formal agreement between the U.S. and Great Britain, which established the border between Canada and southeast Alaska along the mountain divide south from the 141st Meridian to the head of the Portland Canal. This was essentially right where the Mounties had put it.

Chisana Gold Country Left to Wildlife

Alaska Highway, 6.5 miles (10.5 km) north of Yukon border

Information signs about some of the migratory birds found in the Tetlin National Wildlife Refuge can be found at a pullover stop here. In the spring and fall, many of these birds can be seen in the refuge's Chisana Valley, south of the highway at this point. The Chisana Valley was also the scene of a minor gold rush in 1913. The value of gold claims turned out to be small, however, and prospectors abandoned the area almost as fast as they had come, leaving the wilderness to the local wildlife.

In 1980, the United States Congress established the Tetlin National Wildlife Refuge on 730,000 acres (295,431 ha) in eastern Alaska. Here, where the Chisana and Nabesna rivers join to form the Tanana, the forests and peaks of Tetlin surround hundreds of lakes and marshes that tend to thaw early and provide rest stops for wildfowl migrating to nesting sites throughout the Alaska interior. The wildlife refuge also provides a home for the more than 140 species of birds who nest here. Other wildlife species in the area include moose, bear—both black and grizzly—wolf, coyote and red fox. A visitor center, with displays and additional information about the refuge, is located 1 mile (1.3 km) up the road from the stopping point.

Northway Named for Indian Chief
Northway Junction, Alaska Highway, 43 miles (69 km) northwest of Yukon border, then 7 miles (11 km) south on Northway Road

The town of Northway, one of the stopping points on the Northwest Staging Route, was named for Chief Walter Northway, who was thought to be 117 years old at the time of his death in 1993. Chief Northway could remember the first white men ever seen in this area. The men, a group of prospectors, were starving when members of Northway's band found them. The Indians gave the white men food and nursed them back to health.

Tanana River First Mapped by Henry Allan
Historic Milepost 1271, Highway turnout, Alaska Highway, 5 miles (8 km) west of Northway Junction

The Tanana River is the Yukon River's largest tributary. Formed at the nearby confluence of Moose Creek and the Chisana River, it was first explored by Arthur Harper, who was following two Indian guides in 1881. Four years later, the area was mapped by Lieutenant Henry Allan and his men during their expedition through the Alaska interior.

An historical marker at this turnout also notes the importance of Alaska airfields such as the one at nearby Northway.

Built during World War II, these airports connected Alaska with the string of airfields leading south to Edmonton, Alberta, on the Northwest Staging Route. The route was used to bring American planes to Alaska, and from there some were flown to the Soviet Union under a lend-lease agreement that brought the Allied Forces necessary equipment from the United States even before the Americans entered the war.

Dusenberg Construction Company Located at Midway Lake
Historic Milepost 1292, Alaska Highway, 25.5 miles (41 km) west of Northway Junction

A construction camp operated by the E.M. Dusenberg Company was located at Midway Lake during the construction of the Alaska Highway. A U.S. Fish and Wildlife Service interpretive sign at this turnout tells about Wrangell–St. Elias National Park and the native people of Alaska.

Gold Discoveries Responsible for Rise and Decline of Fortymile
Historic Milepost 1306, Tetlin Junction, Alaska Highway, 38 miles (61 km) west of Northway Junction

Tetlin Junction is located at the corner of the Alaska and Taylor highways. Travelers going north take the Taylor to Chicken, Jack Wade and Eagle. Along the way the highway travels through parts of the earliest large mining area in the Yukon watershed, Fortymile River country. At Jack Wade Junction, a turnoff on the Taylor Highway leads over the Top of the World Highway to Dawson City and across the border into the Yukon.

Forty miles (64 km) east of Jack Wade, a turnoff on the Top of the World Highway runs 25 miles more (40 km) to an abandoned bridge over the Fortymile River. A 3-mile (5-km) hike from the bridge leads to the former mining settlement of Fortymile. Now a ghost town, with many of its old buildings still standing among the trees that have reclaimed the site, Fortymile was the first large mining town in Alaska and the Yukon. Although the town was in the Yukon, most of the initial mining activity on the Fortymile River was, like the waterway, on the Alaska side of the international boundary.

Arthur Harper made the first significant gold strike on the Fortymile. In the summer of 1881, Harper and three other men traveled cross-country from an Indian village near present-day Eagle to the Tanana River. Along the way, as they crossed the north branch of the Fortymile, Harper stopped to collect what appeared to be promising samples of sand from the riverbank. He carefully stored the samples in his pack, then continued the journey. When they reached the Tanana, Alaska's third largest river, Harper and his companions set out in traditional moose-hide boats, built by the two Indian members of the party, and traveled for 500 miles (805 km) to the river's mouth on the Yukon.

Here, Harper mailed his sand samples to an assayer in San Francisco. To his surprise, assay results came back the following year showing $20,000 worth of gold to the ton. Harper left for the Fortymile as soon as he got word of the value of his find, but despite repeated efforts he was never able to find the spot where he had dug his sand. As a result the Fortymile's major deposits lay undiscovered for another four years, when Harry Madison and Howard Franklin struck coarse gold diggings on the river.

Their discovery sparked the first large gold rush in the Yukon. By the spring of 1887 several hundred miners had swarmed into the area. Arthur Harper, Al Mayo and Jack McQuesten closed Fort Nelson, their trading post at the mouth of the Stewart River, and Jack McQuesten arrived from San Francisco with supplies to start a trading post at the mouth of the Fortymile. Soon a settlement of miners, a blacksmith shop, a sawmill and at least 10 saloons grew up around McQuesten's store. In 1887 a Church of England mission was established on an island alongside the town. In 1895, when the North-West Mounted Police were assigned to the Yukon, they built Fort Constantine across the river next to John J. Healy's three-year-old trading post, Fort Cuday.

The following year, after George Carmack arrived at Fortymile to register his Klondike claims, miners abandoned the town as quickly as they had abandoned their Stewart River claims 10 years before. A small settlement remained at the mouth of the river well into the 20th century, but like so many other mining towns that once sprouted so quickly along the Yukon, Fortymile was destined to become a ghost town.

"Chicken" Easier to Spell Than "Ptarmigan"
Chicken, 66 miles (106 km) north of Tetlin Junction on Taylor Highway

According to a popular story, the old mining town of Chicken, and the creek from which it took its name, used to be called Ptarmigan, after a grouselike bird common to the area. When the settlement got its first post office and it was time to give the town an official name, nobody could remember how to spell ptarmigan, although they were sure it didn't begin with the letter *t*. Because the miners often humorously referred to ptarmigans as chickens when eating them for dinner, someone suggested they use that name for their community instead. The idea was approved and the town has been Chicken ever since.

Trail Built to Eagle
Eagle, 160 miles (258 km) north of Tetlin Junction

Eagle began as a trading center along the Yukon River. The earliest trading post in the area, largely unsuccessful, was established by the Western Fur and Trading Company in 1880, near the Han Indian settlement of David's Village. As the economy of the Yukon turned from fur trading to gold mining, however, Eagle became one of several communities of miners along the river.

A United States Army post was established here in 1899. In 1900 Judge James Wickersham established the first federal court in the Alaska interior at Eagle. In the early years of the new century a trail was built from Valdez on the Alaska coast north to the Yukon River community. A telegraph line also connected Eagle with Dawson City and, later, Valdez and Fairbanks.

Eagle began to decline with the Tanana Valley gold discoveries after the turn of the century, when Fairbanks became the major town in the Alaska interior. Eagle's population dropped from a high in 1899 of 1,700 people to fewer than 200 in 1903. By the 1939 election, only 26 voters were left to cast their ballots. Many of Eagle's historical buildings still stand today, however, and a walking tour of the town is offered by the Eagle Historical Society.

Tok Named for Creek
Alaska Highway, Tok, 11 miles (18 km) west of Tetlin Junction

Tok takes its name from the nearby creek, but where the creek got its name is another question. A favorite story about its origin maintains that the name dates from the expedition of Lieutenant Henry Allen of the United States Army, who traveled and mapped this area in 1885. According to this tale, when Allen and his native guide reached Tok Creek, Allen pointed to the stream and asked in a loud voice "What is this?" Allen was wondering about the name of the creek, but the guide, knowing enough English to think the question silly, answered, *"Tokai,"* which is the native word for "creek."

The town of Tok began nearly 50 years later as a construction camp during the building of the Alaska Highway. Today, Tok is also the only town in the interior of Alaska through which visitors driving to and from the state have to pass twice. There's no road leaving the interior that doesn't pass through Tok on its way to the Yukon border at Beaver Creek or Boundary, the only two options for leaving Alaska outside the Panhandle. Both the Tok Visitor Center and the Alaska Public Lands Information Center here feature wildlife and Alaskan cultural displays.

Donald MacDonald Father of International Highway
Historic Milepost 1352, turnout on Alaska Highway, 29.5 miles (48 km) west of Tok

Donald MacDonald was an Alaska engineer and early advocate for building a highway between Alaska, southern Canada and the lower 48 states. As early as 1929, two international highway associations were formed, one in Dawson City in the Yukon, the other in Fairbanks, Alaska. Their plan was to lobby the Canadian and American governments to build a road from southern Canada through the Yukon to Alaska. While support was quickly obtained from the northwestern states and British Columbia, the Canadian federal government remained unenthusiastic.

In 1930 a congressional commission undertook a study of proposed highway routes. The result called for a 1,350-mile (2,173-km) route long advocated by MacDonald. This highway would have run from Hazelton, British Columbia, up the eastern side of the Coast Mountains to Dawson City, then west to Fairbanks. The estimated cost was $13,960,000. The most serious disadvantage to the plan, from the Canadian government's point of view, was that approximately $12 million would be for construction inside Canada and presumably paid for by the Canadian government.

MacDonald and other highway advocates continued to press for a northern road, however. In 1938 a second American commission was established, this time with Donald MacDonald as one of its members. Other members included Warren Magnuson, a senator from Washington, and Ernest Gruening, soon-to-be governor of Alaska and a future senator.

A Canadian commission was also appointed at the urging of British Columbia Premier Pattulo. The two commissions met for the first time in July 1939, then again in January 1940. The Americans favored a route known as Plan A along the eastern side of the Coast Mountains mostly because the route would allow access roads to be built to Alaskan coastal communities. The Canadians preferred a route up the Rocky Mountain Trench, which would better serve residents of northern British Columbia and the Yukon.

Before anything could be decided, however, the Japanese bombed Pearl Harbor, and a road that had been primarily of interest to residents of the far northwest suddenly became a national priority for the United States. When the American military chose to build the road far inland from MacDonald's Coast Mountain route, he was bitterly disappointed, but his patriotism tempered his criticisms.

Allen Names Robertson River
Alaska Highway, 32.5 miles (52 km) west of Tok

The bridge on the highway here crosses the Robertson River, named by Lieutenant Henry Trueman Allen for Sergeant Cady Robertson, one of the two men under his command on Allen's expedition to Alaska in 1885—perhaps the United States Army's single most important mapping and exploration in Alaska. The 25-year-old Kentuckian had been sent north by General Nelson Miles to explore Alaska's Copper River country, suspecting that the area might offer a practical American overland route to the Yukon River.

Private Frederick Fickett also accompanied Allen. Although the men had attempted to keep their supplies to a minimum, when they started up the Copper River in late March 1885 their canoes carried several hundred pounds of food, camping equipment and other paraphernalia, including weather monitoring equipment and a camera with glass plates. Soon conditions on the river worsened, and two of the canoes had to be cut in half to make sleds. The men could pull only about 150 pounds (68 kilograms) on each sled, so half their equipment and supplies had to be abandoned.

The expedition continued north until they reached the mouth of the Chitina River on April 10. After spending more than two weeks mapping and exploring the Chitina, Allen continued up the Copper, heading into areas no white man had ever been before, at least so far as was known. Because they had already abandoned most of their supplies, the men had to depend on what they could kill or forage along the way. Had it not been for assistance from native people they occasionally encountered, all three would have starved.

On May 30 at a point that Allen calculated to be 285 miles (459 km) south of the Arctic Circle, the men left the Copper River and headed northeast guided by an Indian who had volunteered to help Allen's expedition. He showed the white men edible roots to eat along the way so they wouldn't starve to death, and then he led them to a small creek where salmon were spawning.

Eventually, the group crossed the Alaska Range at Suslota Pass and descended to the Tanana Valley. By this time Sergeant Robertson was suffering from scurvy. The men built a boat covered with caribou hide at an Indian village on the Tetlin River. From there they drifted downstream to the Tanana River, then down the Tanana to its mouth on the Yukon. Although the Tanana had been known to white men for a number of years, Allen was the first to map its course.

Once Allen and his men reached the Yukon, they waited at a small community called Nuklukayet for a steamer to take Sergeant Robertson on to St. Michael, where he could get a ship back to San Francisco. Meanwhile, Allen and Private Fickett hired Indian guides to take them north to the Koyukuk River. For the next two months the two men explored the Koyukuk from near its headwaters far north of the Arctic Circle to its mouth back on the Yukon. By August, when Allen was at St. Michael waiting for a ship home, he had traveled nearly 2,000 miles (3,219 km) of the Alaska wilderness. He had also made the first complete maps for three major rivers: the Copper, the Tanana and the Koyukuk.

The Rise and Fall of the Alaska Commercial Company
Gerstle River Bridge, Alaska Highway, 78 miles (126 km) west of Tok

The Gerstle River was named by Lieutenant Henry Allen in 1885 to honor Lewis Gerstle, the president of the Alaska Commercial Company. Soon after the American purchase of Alaska in 1867, Hayward M. Hutchinson and several San Francisco partners formed the Alaska Commercial Company and bought out the old Russian-American Company, which was not welcome on Alaskan soil once it became an American possession. Assets of the company included steamers, sailing ships, wharves and even furs left behind in warehouses at Sitka, Kodiak, Unalaska and the Pribilof Islands.

In addition to the lucrative fur seal harvest, the company traded furs along the Yukon River, establishing posts as far inland as Fort Reliance, six miles (10 km) from present-day Dawson City. For 20 years the Alaska Commercial Company ran a virtual monopoly on the Yukon River until John J. Healy's North American Trading and Transportation Company entered the trade in 1892. Both companies ran steamboats between St. Michael and trading posts on the upper river.

The Klondike Gold Rush brought additional independent traders, miners and fortune seekers to the Yukon and more than 30 new trading and transportation companies. Then, in 1900, the completion of the White Pass & Yukon Route railway changed transportation patterns in the North at the same time as the booming gold rush economy began to slow down. This forced many of the new companies out of business, while other companies consolidated or were absorbed by larger companies.

The Alaska Commercial Company joined with several others to form two separate enterprises: the Northern Navigation Company, which continued in the river transportation business, and the Northern Commercial Company, which concentrated on the retail trade. Of all the companies that had operated in Alaska, only the North American Transportation and Trading Company remained a viable competitor for the new companies on the lower Yukon River, and it only lasted a few years more. Meanwhile, the British Yukon Navigation Company, owned by the White Pass & Yukon Route, became the largest competitor on the upper Yukon. Later, it operated on the lower Yukon as the American Yukon Navigation Company. In 1914, this firm bought out its competitor. By this time, however, the New Alaska Railroad had reduced the importance of river traffic on the Yukon. By the 1950s the new all-weather road to Dawson City all but ended commercial traffic on the river.

Fort Cudahy, the North American Transportation and Trading Company post at Fortymile in 1895.

Agriculture Comes to Alaska
University of Alaska Agricultural and Forestry Research Station, Alaska Highway, 93 miles (150 km) west of Tok

In an effort to attract residents and diversify the state's economy by growing more of its own food, the state of Alaska began encouraging agricultural development in the 1970s. While this effort met with only limited success, today barley, oats and forage are grown on approximately 40,000 acres (16,188 ha) of land.

Livestock production is also important to the region and a few area farmers have also experimented successfully with commercial vegetables.

Delta Junction End of Alaska Highway
Richardson and Alaska highways, Delta Junction, 107 miles (172 km) west of Tok

The official end of the Alaska Highway has always been the subject of controversy. Today, Delta Junction is recognized as the end of the Alaska Highway even though the original mandate for the World War II construction project called for a road to end at Fairbanks.

The complicating factor was that in 1942 a road already existed between what we know today as Delta Junction and Fairbanks. Logically, Delta Junction can be considered the northern end of the Alaska Highway. This same logic, though, has never been applied to the southern end of the road. When construction began in 1942, there was already a road from Dawson Creek to Charley Lake in British Columbia, but Dawson Creek continues to be considered the official start of the highway.

Original mileages were calculated between Dawson Creek and Fairbanks. At the time the pioneer road was completed in 1942, the Alaska Highway stretched for more than 1,600 miles (2,575 km). As improvements have been made, the road has gradually shortened. Today, only about 1,400 miles (2,253 km) of road exist between Dawson Creek and Delta Junction.

Today, Alaska Highway travelers complete their trip to Fairbanks on the Richardson Highway. The Richardson was built between Fairbanks and Valdez on the Alaska coast 30 years before the Alaska Highway. The first automobile to drive the Richardson did so in 1913, but dog trains had used the trail as early as 1902. The road began in 1899 as a military route between Valdez and Eagle, before Fairbanks had even been established. After gold strikes in the Tanana Valley spurred growth there, however, the trail was redirected to the new town of Fairbanks.

Delta Junction Originally Called Buffalo Center
Richardson and Alaska highways, Delta Junction, Visitor Center

The town of Delta Junction developed from a construction camp established during the building of the Alaska Highway. An earlier settlement at this location was known as Buffalo Center. That name stemmed from the 28 buffalo that were released in the area during the 1920s in a U.S. government attempt to create a free-ranging Alaska buffalo herd. The experiment succeeded and today about 400 animals roam the surrounding countryside, sometimes to the detriment of local farmers. Other free-ranging buffalo can sometimes be seen in smaller numbers closer to Fairbanks.

Rika's Roadhouse at Big Delta State Historical Park
Richardson–Alaska Highway, Big Delta State Historical Park, 9 miles (15 km) west of Delta Junction

Rika's Roadhouse on the Tanana River at Big Delta is one of only two remaining roadhouses on the old Valdez-to-Fairbanks trail. In the early years of the century there were at least 30 along the road. The original roadhouse on this site was built in 1904. Sometime in the early years a Swedish immigrant named Rika Wallen began working there, and in 1923 she bought the property for $10 plus the money owed her by her employer, John Hajdukovich, for several years' back wages. Hajdukovich had started the roadhouse in 1904, but Wallen had run the place for a number of years before she bought it. Rumors at the time had it that Wallen had once had a romantic relationship with Hajdukovich. Wallen never married. She operated the roadhouse until almost midcentury and after retiring continued to live there until her death in 1969. Today, Wallen's homestead and roadhouse, including a small museum with exhibits dating from the building of the Alaska Highway, are located in the state park.

Alyeska Pipeline Crosses River
Big Delta Bridge, Richardson–Alaska Highway, 99.5 miles (160 km) west of Delta Junction

A highway view stop here offers a spectacular view of the huge Alyeska Pipeline suspended from its bridge across the Tanana River. Built in the 1970s, the $8 billion pipeline, carrying oil from Prudhoe Bay on the Arctic Ocean across the state to Valdez on the southern coast was the largest privately funded business project in history. Since that time, Prudhoe Bay oil has funneled huge amounts of money into Alaska's economy.

The Alaskan oil boom has, however, come with an environmental price. Although extensive studies were carried out before the project was allowed to proceed and despite many precautions designed to protect the northern caribou, the pipeline appears to have permanently divided the northern herd. And while no major spills have occurred on the pipeline itself, thousands of barrels of Prudhoe Bay oil were spilled by the tanker *Exxon Valdez* into Prince William Sound in 1989. Millions of dollars were spent cleaning up the area, but much of the destruction to the pristine environment of Prince William Sound was irreparable. Today, the mishap can only serve as a reminder of the sometimes terrible costs of modern technology.

Santa Finds New Home
North Pole, Alaska, Richardson–Alaska Highway, 83 miles (134 km) west of Delta Junction

North Pole, Alaska, was named with the expressed intention of luring a southern toy company north to manufacture toys and thereby stimulate the local economy. Today, community businesses promote the popular version of the Christmas spirit in the little town of North Pole all year long. With Christmas cards and decorations everywhere, shopping in North Pole is like visiting a favorite mall on Christmas Eve, no matter what the actual season. At North Pole, tourists buy Christmas presents all year long.

Felix Pedro Founds Fairbanks
Richardson–Alaska Highway, Fairbanks, 98 miles (158 km) west of Delta Junction

Italian prospector Felix Pedro is usually credited with being the founder of Fairbanks. It was he who, after prospecting in the area and making good strikes, advised E.T. Barnette in 1901 to open a trading post on the Chena River rather than at Tanana Crossing. Barnette expected a town to grow up around his trading post, and he promised Alaska Judge James Wickersham that he would call it Fairbanks after Wickersham's friend Senator Charles Warren Fairbanks of Indiana.

After Barnette built his store he did everything he could to encourage other prospectors to come to the area. Except for a minor gold rush after he sent word of Pedro's strike to Dawson in 1901, the Tanana Valley didn't attract much attention until 1903. Then, additional gold finds brought miners swarming to the area. It inspired Judge Wickersham, who arranged to have an Alaskan courthouse built in Fairbanks, to write that he hoped Fairbanks would one day "become an American Dawson City." By 1904 Fairbanks boasted nearly 400 log buildings and over 1,000 residents, with about the same number living along nearby creeks.

By 1915 gold dredges were operating in the Tanana region, with the large mining companies keeping Fairbanks prosperous for a number of years after the placer mines of the original prospectors had been worked out. Then, wartime construction, the nearby military base and the Alaska Highway brought new wealth to the area. Through the 1950s the Distant Early Warning Line (the DEW Line) and other military projects were important to the local economy, as was the University of Alaska. Fairbanks also became the service center for the Arctic regions of Alaska and, in the 1970s, a center for activities during the construction of the Alyeska Pipeline from Prudhoe Bay to Valdez.

Blue Parka Man Robs Bishop
Courthouse Square, Cushman Street and Second Avenue, Fairbanks

The gold rush that established the city of Fairbanks has sometimes been called the first modern gold rush because settling Fairbanks was an essentially orderly and civilized affair, with little of the lawlessness that characterized many of the state's previous gold rush camps. By the time of the Fairbanks stampede, civil law had been established in Alaska and the stampeders themselves were, for the most part, experienced sourdoughs with fewer of the lawless camp followers so common in earlier stampedes.

Perhaps, just as importantly, Fairbanks was a different kind of gold rush than others. Gold deposits here lay deeper in the ground. Mining them required bigger and more expensive equipment, and extraction took longer. People realized that instead of the boom-and-bust economy normally found in placer deposits of the North the new town of Fairbanks would be around indefinitely. Men brought their families to stay. Businesses opened with the expectation of remaining open for years to come. Crime was no more a problem here than in similar-sized communities in the south.

There were, of course, enough exceptions to the law-abiding nature of most of Fairbanks' citizens for the new community to establish a courthouse and jail. The old courthouse that houses the shops and offices of Courthouse Square today was originally built in 1933. An earlier jail on the same site was established in 1903 by the first judge in Fairbanks, James Wickersham. Perhaps the most famous criminal trial in early Fairbanks was Elbridge Barnette, the man who opened the first trading post here and promoted a local gold rush to the area even before he had any real evidence that gold could be found here.

Once the stampede brought people to the region, Barnette sold his trading post to the Alaska Commercial Company and started a bank. Barnette's bank appeared to everyone to be thriving, but in 1911 it suddenly closed. People all over town lost their savings. Everyone blamed Barnette. Apparently, he had been embezzling money from his own bank, leaving nearly a million dollars of depositors' funds unaccounted for. Evidence against him was circumstantial, however, and Barnette was eventually convicted only of the minor charge of filing false bank statements. Fined a thousand dollars, he hurriedly left town.

Perhaps, a more representative crook in early Fairbanks was the highway robber known as the Blue Parka Man. The Blue Parka Man stalked the main trail into Fairbanks. During his robberies, he always wore a blue parka pulled over his head to hide his identity. What was truly noteworthy about the robber, however, was his courtesy and friendliness toward his victims.

The best-known story about the Blue Parka Man involved Peter Trimble Rowe, the Episcopal bishop in Fairbanks. Once robbed along the trail with a group of other victims, the bishop was suddenly singled out by the Blue Parka Man and asked if he weren't a minister in Fairbanks. Yes, said Rowe, he was the bishop of the local Episcopal Church. "I thought so," said the Blue Parka Man. "Take your poke back off that pile in the road, Bishop. In fact, take a couple of pokes off the pile. I'm a member of your church." Two years later, when the Blue Parka Man was finally captured he, indeed, turned out to be a local Episcopalian.

Circle Becomes Largest Log Cabin City in World
Steese Highway, Fairbanks

The Steese Highway, connecting Fairbanks with Circle City, a mining town about 50 miles (80 km) from the Arctic Circle and 167 miles (269 km) northeast of Fairbanks, was built in the 1920s. Circle, so named because early prospectors thought it situated on the Arctic Circle, was one of the earliest gold camps in the Yukon Valley. A settlement built around Jack McQuesten's trading post started here in 1893 when gold was discovered on nearby Birch Creek.

Within a few months, the mines on Birch Creek and nearby streams were extracting some $400,000 worth of gold a year. By 1896, twelve hundred people lived in Circle and miners called it the Paris of the North. *The Chicago Daily Record* called it the "largest log town in the world." The town even sported an opera house that featured plays and vaudeville shows, although its limited repertoire meant that the same routines had to be performed over and over again during the long Alaska winter.

Circle appeared to be the most promising gold mining town along the Yukon, but in the winter of 1896–97 rumors began to filter in about a huge strike upstream on a river they were calling the Thorndike. Just before Christmas in 1896 two traders brought a letter that was read in a Circle saloon. Gold, the letter said, was sometimes running $150 a pan or even higher. The miners, who had heard that kind of talk before, laughed heartily and ordered more drinks, although a few left quietly for the gold fields of Dawson. Then in January 1897 more mail arrived from the new town of Dawson, including a letter to Harry Ash, who owned the Circle City saloon, where the crowd had ignored news of the new strike the previous month.

This time Ash received a letter from Bill McPhee, a saloon keeper at Fortymile and a trusted friend. The letter told Ash that the rumors he had been hearing from Dawson were true. The strike was the richest ever. Ash read the letter to himself, then jumped over the bar. "Boys," he said to the crowd in his saloon as he ran for the door, "take what you want. I'm off to the Klondike."

Although a few men stayed in Circle long enough to clean out the saloon, the town turned into a virtual ghost town almost overnight. Suddenly, the log cabins once valued at several hundred dollars each were worth nothing—although a good dog sled could get its owner a thousand or more. Unlucky prospectors began returning to Circle within a few months, but the town would never again be referred to as the biggest log town in the world or as the Paris of Alaska.

DIRECTORY OF MUSEUMS

Alaska

Adak

Adak Community Museum

Anaktuvuk Pass

Simon Paneak Memorial
Museum
341 Mekiana Road

Anchorage

Alaska Aviation Heritage
Museum
4721 Aircraft Drive
Lake Hood

Alaska Humanities Forum
430 West Seventh Avenue,
Suite 1

Alaska State Council on the Arts
411 West 4th Avenue, Suite 1E

Alaska Zoo
4731 O'Malley Road

Anchorage Museum of History
& Art
121 West 7th Avenue

Heritage Library and Museum
National Bank of Alaska
301 W. Northern Lights Boule-
vard

The Imaginarium
5th Avenue between G & H
Streets

National Park Service
2525 Gambell Street

Oscar Anderson House
420 M Street

Bethel

Yupiit Piciryarait Cultural
Center and Museum

Central

Circle Historical Museum
Milepost 128, Steese Highway

Copper Center

George I. Ashby Memorial
Museum/Copper Valley
Historical Society
Milepost 101, Old Richardson
Highway
Copper Center Loop Road

Cordova

Cordova Historical Museum
622 First Street (Centennial
Building)

Denali Park

Denali National Park

Dillingham

Samuel K. Fox Museum
Corner of Seward & D Streets

Eagle

Eagle Pioneer Museum/Eagle
Historical Society
Eagle's Historic District

Eagle River

Southcentral Alaska Museum
of Natural History (SAMONH)
Parkgate Building

Fairbanks

Fairbanks Visitor Information
Center
1st Avenue and Cushman
Street
*An historic walking tour of
downtown Fairbanks begins
and ends at this sod-roofed log-
cabin information center on the
corner of First Avenue and
Cushman Street. Information
and maps of the walk are available at the center. The complete
tour, which takes at least a couple of hours to finish and
includes many of Fairbanks'
earliest homes and businesses,
takes visitors past the old red-*
*light district, the Clay Street
Cemetery and the Empress Theater. Information about an historical driving tour of Fairbanks and the surrounding
area can also be obtained at the
Visitor Information Center.*

Steamboat Landing Trading
Post
Discovery Drive
*Alaska's only operating
sternwheeler,* Discovery III, *
takes visitors from its dock in
Fairbanks on regularly sched-
uled tours of the Chena and
Tanana rivers.*

University of Alaska Fairbanks
Museum
907 Yukon Drive
*The University Museum fea-
tures Alaskan historical
exhibits and programs, including a large number aboriginal
cultural displays. A 36,000-
year-old bison, removed from
permafrost near Fairbanks, is
on display along with
dinosaur fossils and other
archaeological exhibits.*

Public Lands Information
Center
3rd Avenue and Cushman
Street
*This museum and informa-
tion center features material
about Alaskan natural history,
aboriginal history and outdoor
recreational activities. Infor-*

mational films and interpretive programs are offered. A small book store is also located here.

Alaskaland Pioneer Park
Alaskaland Park, Airport Way
   This theme park mixes historical information with a good time. Displays include historic buildings once part of downtown Fairbanks, an art gallery, native exhibits and an aviation museum. A musical comedy is performed nightly at the Palace Saloon.

Fairbanks Dog Mushing Museum
250 Cushman Street
Courthouse Square, Suite 2B
   Exhibits focus on the history of dog mushing in Alaska.

Alaska Native Village Museum/
Fairbanks Native Association
Alaskaland Park, Airport Way

Pioneer Memorial Park Inc.
Alaskaland Park, Airport Way

Wickersham House Museum/
Tanana-Yukon Historical Society
Alaskaland Park, Airport Way

Fort Nelson

Fort Nelson Heritage Museum
Alaska Highway
   Located across the highway

from the travel information center, the Fort Nelson Heritage Museum is one of the most attractive and interesting museums on the highway. Displays include pioneer, wildlife and Alaska Highway artifacts as well as antique vehicles, a large collection of machinery and a trapper's cabin.

Haines

Alaska Indian Arts
#23 Fort Seward Drive

Sheldon Museum & Cultural Center
Corner of Main & 1st Streets

Homer

Pratt Museum/Homer Society of Natural History
3779 Bartlett Street

Huslia

Huslia Cultural Center
Next to City Office

Juneau

Alaska State Museum
395 Whittier Street

House of Wickersham
213 7th Street

Juneau Douglas City Museum
4th & Main Streets

Kake Tribal Heritage
Foundation
Kake Tribal Corporation
93009 Glacier Highway

Kenai

Kenai Bicentennial Visitors &
Cultural Center
11471 Kenai Spur Highway

Kenaitze Indian Tribe, IRA
2255 Ames Street

Ketchikan

Tongass Historical Museum
629 Dock Street

Totem Heritage Center
601 Deermont Street
907-225-5900

Kodiak

Alutiiq Culture Center/Kodiak
Area Native Association
214 W. Rezanof Drive

Baranov Museum/
Kodiak Historical Society
101 Marine Way

Kotzebue

NANA Museum of the Arctic
100 Shore Avenue

Metlakatla

Duncan Cottage Museum

Duncan Street

Nome

Carrie McLain Memorial
Museum
200 E. Front Street

Palmer

Palmer Museum/Chamber of
Commerce
723 So. Valley Way

Petersburg

Clausen Memorial Museum
203 Fram Street

Seward

Resurrection Bay Historical
Society
336 3rd Avenue

Sitka

Isabel Miller Museum/Sitka
Historical Society
330 Harbor Drive

Russian Bishop's House
Lincoln Street

Sheldon Jackson Museum
104 College Drive

Sitka National Historical Park
106 Metlakatla Street

Southeast Alaska Indian Cul-

tural Center
106 Metlakatla Street

Skagway

Arctic Brotherhood Hall
Visitor Center
Broadway Street
It has been reported that this hall, an 1899 building fronted with over 10,000 pieces of driftwood, is the most photographed building in Alaska. There are a few local history exhibits and photographs on display here. The Arctic Brotherhood was a fraternal organization of Alaska and Yukon pioneers that began at an informal meeting of 11 men on a steamer trip between Seattle and Skagway in 1899. Soon the organization grew to include 30 branches throughout the Yukon and Alaska. The last member to be initiated into the Skagway club was President Warren Harding on his 1923 visit to Alaska.

Klondike National Historical
Park Visitor Center
2nd Avenue and Broadway
Street
The visitor center here features displays, films and talks about Klondike and Skagway history. Walking tours are scheduled throughout the day during the summer months. Chilkoot Trail information is

also available. The Klondike National Historic Park includes the Skagway historic district, the Chilkoot and White Pass trails, and Pioneer Square in Seattle, Washington. In Skagway, many of the buildings in town date back to the gold rush era. These range from the tiny compartments of the red-light district (now turned into gift shops) to the old White Pass & Yukon Route railway offices that have become the headquarters of the National Historical Park. New buildings constructed in the district also, by law, are built to conform to turn-of-the-century architecture.

Skagway Historical Museum
and Archives
7th Avenue and Spring Street
Located on the second floor of the former Skagway courthouse, this museum focuses on Skagway history at the time of the Klondike Gold Rush. Displays include artifacts and photographs of the gold rush days, including White Pass & Yukon Route railway exhibits and a faro table from a local saloon. There are also displays of early commerce, native people and miners as well as an archival collection of historical documents. The museum building was built as a school by the Methodist Church in

1899. *The following year public education came to Alaska, so the building was sold to the federal government. For half a century it was used as a courthouse and jail. Then in* 1956 *the city of Skagway bought the building to use as a city hall. The museum opened in* 1961.

Corrington Museum of Alaskan History
5th Avenue and Broadway Street

Scrimshawed (hand-engraved) walrus tusks and other ivory carvings depict the history of the state at the Corrington Museum. Exhibits trace Alaskan history from the era of the Bering land bridge to the 20th century. Native culture, whaling, trapping and the mining frontiers are all represented. The museum operates inside Corrington's gift store.

Mascot Saloon
3rd Avenue and Broadway Street
The Mascot Saloon, a barroom restored by the National Park Service in 1990, *features exhibits about life in Skagway during the gold rush.*

Soldotna

Soldotna Historical Society &

Museum, Inc.
Centennial Park Road

Sutton

Alpine Historical Park
Milepost 61.5 Glenn Highway

Talkeetna

Talkeetna Historical Society
Downtown Talkeetna

Tok

University of Alaska Agricultural and Forestry Research Station
Alaska Highway, 93 miles (150 km) west of Tok
Twelve miles (19 km) west of the entrance to the agricultural research station and about a mile (.6 km) down a side road to the south, the Alaska Homestead and Historical Museum offers visitors a look at early agriculture in the North. Museum exhibits include historical farming, logging and mining equipment as well as working displays that include farm animals, greenhouses, hay fields and gardens.

Valdez

Valdez Museum & Historical Archive
217 Egan Drive

Wasilla

Dorothy Page Museum & Old
Wasilla Townsite Park
323 Main Street

Museum of Alaska Trans-
portation & Industry
Milepost 46.5, Parks Highway

Wasilla-Knik-Willow Creek
Historical Society
323 Main Street

Wrangell

Wrangell Historical
Society/Museum
122 2nd Street

Yukon

Burwash Landing

Kluane Museum
Alaska Highway

Carcross

Frontierland
Klondike Highway, 1.5 miles
(2.4 km) north of Carcross
*Built around a frontier
theme, some excellent Yukon
wildlife displays can be found
here, including the world's
largest mounted bear (a polar
bear).*

Dawson City

Dawson City Museum
Fifth Avenue & Church Street

*The Dawson City Museum,
the oldest museum in the
Yukon, documents the life of
early Dawson, the gold rush
era of 1896–99, and European
and aboriginal history in the
Yukon Territory before the
great stampede. The first
Dawson City Museum was set
up in the town library in 1901.
By the 1950s, the community's
museum was housed in the
firehall. This building was
destroyed—taking the museum's contents with it—in a fire
in 1959.*

*Today's Dawson City Muse-
um is located in the old Territorial Administration Building, which dates from 1901,
when Dawson was the capital
of the Yukon. After the seat of
government for the territory
was moved to Whitehorse in
1953, the building took on a
number of different roles
before becoming the new town
museum in 1962.*

Keno City

Keno City Mining Museum
Milepost 70, North Klondike
Highway

Mayo

Binet House Interpretive
Centre
Silver Trail, 32 miles (52 km)
northeast of Klondike Highway
*This community museum
features a collection of photographs, geological displays
and artifacts of early community life.*

Teslin

George Johnston Museum
*The George Johnston Muse-
um is an exceptional local
museum operated by the Teslin
Historical Museum Society. In
addition to an exhibit of Johnston's 1928 Chevrolet, the museum includes a well-displayed
collection of early Yukon memorabilia and Tlingit cultural
artifacts. Photographs from
George Johnston's collection
displayed here offer visitors a
rare look at Tlingit history and
life in early Teslin.*

Watson Lake

The Alaska Highway
Interpretive Centre
Behind the Signpost Forest
Junction of the Alaska and
Robert Campbell Highways
*Slide show, videos and dis-
plays at the interpretive center
deal, for the most part, with*
*the construction of the Alaska
Highway and the airfields
along the Northwest Staging
Route. A visitor information
center is also located here.*

Whitehorse

SS *Klondike* National Historic
Site, next to the Robert
Campbell Bridge
*The Yukon River stern-
wheeler SS Klondike, refurbished by Parks Canada, is
open for visitors every day
throughout the summer. A film
on the history of riverboat traffic is shown daily in an adjacent tent theater, and tours of
the craft are scheduled every
half hour.*
The Yukon Transportation
Museum
Alaska Highway
*The Yukon Transportation
Museum, on the Alaska Highway near the Whitehorse Airport, concentrates on exhibits
about transportation in the
Yukon. Exhibits range from
those related to the Alaska
Highway, to aircraft commonly flown in the north, to railroads and even dog sleds and
snowshoes—the traditional
transportation used on early
Yukon trails.*
*Three cairns near the muse-
um's front door commemorate
the construction of the Alaska
Highway and its eventual con-*

trol, first by the Canadian Army, then by civilian authorities.

The MacBride Museum
1st Avenue and Wood Street
The Yukon's premier museum, the MacBride, features cultural and natural history displays. Here, you will find a cabin built by the real Sam McGee, Mounted Police exhibits, gold rush relics, audio-visual displays and much more.

The Old Church Museum
Third Avenue and Elliot Street
Built in 1900, this restored log church features relics and photographs from early Yukon missions.
LePage Park
3rd Avenue and Wood Street
This small park features three restored buildings typical of Whitehorse homes in the years immediately following the Klondike Gold Rush. Other examples of early architecture in Whitehorse can be seen by taking one of the walking tours that leave from Donnenworth House, 3126 Third Avenue, at regular intervals throughout the summer.
Yukon Historical & Museums Association
3126 3rd Avenue, next to Lepage Park

British Columbia

Dawson Creek

Dawson Creek Station Museum
Alaska Avenue
Housed in an old Northern Alberta Railway station, the museum contains railroad, pioneer and wildlife displays. A visitor information center is also located here.

Walter Wright Pioneer Village
Alaska Avenue
The grounds here contain a number of early local buildings, including a log house, a general store and blacksmith shop. Farm machinery and early tools are also on display.

Fort St. John

North Peace Museum
This museum contains pioneer and aboriginal artifacts, with a reconstructed trapper's cabin and schoolhouse. An oil derrick next to the museum recounts the area's more recent history of gas and oil discoveries. A visitor information center is also located here.

Subject Index

Entries are filed word by word.

About the Author

TED STONE has been traveling the North American West for more than twenty years. He is the author of *Alberta History Along the Highway* and the editor of the bestselling *Riding the Northern Range: Poems From the Last Best-West, 100 Years of Cowboy Stories* and *A Roundup of Cowboy Humor.* Ted Stone's own bestselling stories include *Hailstorms & Hoop Snakes* and *It's Hardly Worth Talking If You're Going to Tell the Truth.*